# Experience Your Bible

## JOSH McDOWELL
## SEAN McDOWELL

## HARVEST HOUSE PUBLISHERS
EUGENE, OREGON

*Cover by Koechel Peterson & Associates, Inc., Minneapolis, Minnesota*

*Cover photo © Koechel Peterson & Associates, Inc.*

**EXPERIENCE YOUR BIBLE**
Copyright © 2012 by Josh McDowell Ministry and Sean McDowell
Published by Harvest House Publishers
Eugene, Oregon 97402
www.harvesthousepublishers.com

Library of Congress Cataloging-in-Publication Data
    McDowell, Josh.
    Experience your Bible / Josh McDowell and Sean McDowell.
        p. cm.
    Includes bibliographical references.
    ISBN 978-0-7369-2873-1 (pbk.)
    ISBN 978-0-7369-4133-4 (eBook)
    1. Bible—Criticism, interpretation, etc. I. McDowell, Sean. II. Title.
    BS511.3.M337 2012
    220.6'1—dc23

                                                                    2011022066

*To Dr. Robert Saucy of Talbot Theological Seminary*

*Thank you for giving us a love for the Scriptures,
for teaching us how to understand the Bible,
and for personally pouring yourself into each of our lives.*

## Acknowledgments

We wish to recognize the following individuals for their valuable contribution to this book.

Dave Bellis, my (Josh's) friend and colleague for 35 years, for collaborating with us on the outline of the book, writing the first draft, and rewriting and doing the overall shaping of this work into its final form. In many respects, we consider Dave a "third author" and are deeply grateful for his contribution.

Dr. David Ferguson, for his insights and ministry in our own lives, especially in regard to his focus on relational theology and experiencing the Bible. David's ministry through the Great Commandment Network has impacted many lives through his sermons and printed material, and his ministry impact is reflected in the many pages of this book.

Dr. Richard Fisher, for critiquing the manuscript and providing a wealth of biblical knowledge and insights into interpreting Scripture.

The Niemi small group for providing helpful input and guidance to the book manuscript as they used the material for their group study. Also to Mark and Marcie Niemi, Kathryn and Andy Milligan, and Laura Fahringer for reviewing the manuscript and providing insights that helped us make the book more clear and easier to understand.

Tom Williams, for editing the manuscript, to which he applied his valuable wordsmithing skills and passionate heart to make words come alive on a printed page.

Becky Bellis, for laboring long and hard at the computer to ready the manuscript.

Dave Bellis II, for his insights into the book of Hosea and the added passion he brought to this work in pursuing God's Word with a heart of relational discovery.

Terry Glaspey of Harvest House, for his analytical skills and structural understanding of what makes for a compelling book, and for sharing them to help form the direction of this book.

Paul Gossard of Harvest House, for the expert editing and insight he brought to the manuscript completion.

Bob Hawkins Jr. and the Harvest House Publishers team, who caught the vision of experiencing your Bible and labored with us to bring this book to reality.

*Josh McDowell*
*Sean McDowell*

# Contents

CHAPTER 1: The Bible: Mysterious and Hard
to Understand? .......................... 9

**PART ONE**
**WAYS THE BIBLE IS EXPERIENCED**

CHAPTER 2: The Forgotten Purpose of Scripture .......... 21

CHAPTER 3: Opening the Eyes of Our Hearts ........... 37

CHAPTER 4: Experiencing Jesus in Scripture .............. 51

CHAPTER 5: Experiencing Scripture with Others .......... 63

CHAPTER 6: The Key to Discovering the Truth ............ 77

**PART TWO**
**HOW TO EXPERIENCE THE BIBLE FOR YOURSELF**

CHAPTER 7: Interpretation: Understanding
the Intended Meaning .................... 91

CHAPTER 8: Tools of Interpretation ................... 105

CHAPTER 9: Sharing Your Insights with Others .......... 125

CHAPTER 10: "Go and Learn the Meaning of
This Scripture" .......................... 137

CHAPTER 11: Placing Yourself Within the Big Picture
of Scripture ............................ 147

CHAPTER 12: Why You Can Trust the Bible ............. 163

A Final Word ........................... 179

Additional Resources ..................... 183

Notes .................................. 197

Chapter 1

# The Bible: Mysterious and Hard to Understand?

*"I love the Bible and I believe it is God's Word, but to be honest I don't understand a lot of what it means."*

*"I feel guilty for not reading the Bible more, but the reality is the Bible is somewhat confusing to me, and a lot of it just doesn't relate."*

The above comments represent the thinking of many Christians today. Let's face it—the Bible isn't always an easy read. To a large number of believers many of the 66 books of the Old and New Testament are complex and a little intimidating. This is not surprising, because most of the original Scripture came out of times and cultures vastly different from ours. The Bible was written over 2000 years ago through more than 40 generations by more than 40 different authors from every walk of life. It was penned on the continents of Asia, Africa, and Europe in three languages: Hebrew, Aramaic, and Greek. So it is little wonder that we can feel a little confused by the language and culture of Bible times. Even when Jesus walked the earth, his disciples, who lived in the same society he did, struggled to understand the meaning and relevance of some Scriptures written long before their own time and culture. Let's look briefly at one example of this confusion.

## MAKING THE UNCLEAR, CLEAR

It had been an emotional and confusing day. As the two disciples walked the seven miles from Jerusalem to the village of Emmaus, they tried to sort things out. They thought Jesus had come as their Messiah to rescue Israel from the oppression of the Romans. Those hopes were dashed, of course, when he had been taken by the Romans and crucified.

It was confusing enough to think that your Messiah was going to deliver you and then watch as he gave himself up to be crucified. Now even more confusing were the reports that had been circulating all morning. The women who had gone to Jesus' tomb had found the stone rolled away and his body gone. They said angel-like men had told them Jesus had risen from the dead. Peter had gone to check their story out and confirmed that the tomb was empty. What were they to make of all this?

As they walked and talked a stranger joined them. After listening to what they were saying, he asked, "What are you two talking about?" Amazed, one of them, Cleopas, retorted, "You must be the only person in Jerusalem who hasn't heard about all these things." The stranger asked, "What things?"

The two then told their new "uninformed friend" about Jesus—his life, death, and reported resurrection. At that point the stranger began to explain everything the Scripture said and meant about this man called Jesus, the true Messiah.

When they arrived at their destination the two invited their friend to join them for supper and stay the night. When this stranger broke bread, blessed it, and began giving it to them, their eyes and hearts were opened. Astonished, they recognized this stranger as none other than Jesus—their resurrected Lord. And then he vanished before their very eyes. "They asked each other, 'Were not our hearts burning within us while he talked with us on the road and opened the Scriptures to us?'" (Luke 24:32 NIV).

The Scriptures Jesus quoted to his two followers on the road to Emmaus were not new. Those disciples had heard those passages many times before, yet they had missed their true meaning and relevance. But this time when Jesus "opened the Scriptures" to them, their hearts were opened with new insight and relevance. Isn't that what we all long for—a time when the meaning of God's Word becomes so clear that it meets our needs, gives direction to our life, and provides practical insight for living?

---

God meant his Book to be your personal journey to discover how you were meant to live and enjoy life to the fullest.

---

Here's a valid question: Why would God give us a book with all its promised wisdom and understanding of life and make it difficult to comprehend? If the Bible has relevant truth, why is it so hard to extract its relevance to our lives? Some conclude that the Book is a theological treatise written for religious experts. It's their task to break it down, preach it, and explain its meaning to us.

The problem with leaving the explanation of Scripture to the "experts" is that we miss the real and personal value of discovering its hidden treasures ourselves. Jesus said when a pearl merchant "discovered a pearl of great value, he sold everything he owned and bought it!" (Matthew 13:46). The true meaning and relevance of God's truth is of great value, and discovering it yourself will make all the difference in the world. God has packed his Book with gems of truth just for you, each to be experienced in just the right situation and at just the right time in your life. His Book is his love letters written from his heart to yours. And he never intended his message to be confusing or complex or given to you secondhand. In fact, he meant his Book to be your personal journey to discover how you were meant to live and enjoy life to the fullest.

I (Sean, Josh's son and co-author) am an educator at a Christian high school. I wanted to introduce my students to the Bible as a journey into what God wants to say to them personally and collectively. I printed out the entire book of Ephesians with the chapter numbers, verse numbers, and headings removed. Paul wrote Ephesians as a letter to the church at Ephesus and, quite obviously, it did not originally contain chapter divisions, section headings, and verse numbers. With these things removed, the students could see the letter in a form much closer to the original and come to their own conclusions about its structure and meaning. While chapters and verses are helpful in some respects, they often cause us to focus on the particulars and miss the larger point.

The first thing I had my students do was read the entire book in one sitting without taking any notes. I told them to focus on the big picture of Ephesians and not get lost in the details. This was the first time some of them had ever read an entire book of the Bible straight through. It took about 20 minutes. Then we briefly discussed the central ideas of Ephesians, like why Paul wrote this letter and to whom was he writing it. I simply asked them what they had learned by reading the book straight through.

The next day we began class by reading Ephesians again in its entirety. I told them to focus on what is repeated throughout the book so they could pick up on important themes and trends. This time I let them take notes. Afterward, I asked them what they had learned about the church at Ephesus just by reading the book. They began to uncover topics like works, grace, forgiveness, what it means to be children of God, and so on.

The third day we read the letter through out loud, popcorn style, going around the room with each person reading three verses, one right after the other. Then I asked what they learned by hearing it instead of reading it silently. I also pressed them to share what big ideas they saw in both its structure and ideas.

The fourth day they read Ephesians silently again. Then I put them in groups to work out a summary statement of the whole book. On subsequent days I guided them to break the book down into chapters and subchapters and come up with a heading for each of them. These students were amazed that through this easy process they could find so much depth and relevance—even in a single verse. And they began to realize that these gems of truth were relevant to their own lives. (You can see what my students came up with at the end of the book under "Additional Resources.")

In this book we want to provide you with a simple methodology that will bring clarity and meaning to the stories and parables of Scripture and what God is saying to us in his Word. But in addition, we want you to go beyond mere study of Scripture to mine out its gems of truth to actually experiencing the Bible. By *experience* we mean unlocking the hidden meanings of God's truth so that his ways and life resonate throughout your own life. The Bible is living and active, and his words are there to infuse you with godly understanding, wisdom, meaning, fulfillment, and joy. And all these transforming insights are the workings of God's Spirit.

## ENLIGHTENED BY THE SPIRIT OF TRUTH

"No one can know God's thoughts," Paul says, "except God's own Spirit. And God has actually given us his Spirit (not the world's spirit) so we can know the wonderful things God has freely given us" (1 Corinthians 2:11-12 NLT). Jesus is no longer here physically to open the Scripture to us as he did for his disciples on the Emmaus road, but he has given us the Holy Spirit, who can perform the same function. We need such help not because the Bible is a book of riddles but because, as Paul said, only God can infuse our finite minds with his infinite wisdom. Unless we are guided by the miraculous person of the Holy Spirit, we will never understand how to navigate through God's Word, and we will miss its transforming meaning and relational significance to our lives.

While it is true that the Holy Spirit is there to open our minds and hearts to what he wants us to know, it isn't as simple as saying, "Speak to me, God, and I will understand." This is a misguided approach to understanding God's truth, and it will lead and has led to disastrous results. We must study and mine out the truths of God's Word. If the Holy Spirit were the sole guide to truth, we wouldn't need the Bible, let alone gifted expositors of the Word, commentaries, multiple translations, Bible software, or a book like this one.

In many respects, the Holy Spirit has a specific vocabulary, and that vocabulary is the Word of God. That means the Holy Spirit will never prompt us to think, say, or do anything in contradiction to his Word.

So the more we study the words of Scripture, the more the Holy Spirit can reveal its meaning and enable us to experience his truth in our lives. But unless we are careful to follow a proven path of interpreting the Bible's meaning, we are vulnerable to false teachings.

There is good reason Paul challenged us to "be diligent [in]...accurately handling the word of truth" (2 Timothy 2:15 NASB). There are false teachers out there, and the enemy doesn't want you to understand God's Book and discern its transforming meaning and significance to your life. Paul warned the church at Corinth of false teachers who "have fooled you by disguising themselves as apostles of Christ. But I am not surprised! Even Satan can disguise himself as an angel of light" (2 Corinthians 11:13-14 NLT). So throughout this book we will explain how to use proven tools and methods to "accurately handle the word of truth."

## APPLICATION PLUS EXPERIENCE

Is the Bible really a mysterious and hard-to-understand book? It is in fact mysterious, because it unlocks the mind and heart and ways of God. But the Word of God is not hard to understand when we know how to use some basic navigational tools for illuminating its meaning.

I (Josh) wrote a book 30 years ago called *Guide to Understanding Your Bible*. It outlined my own personal study method for unlocking the truths of God's Word. This book is drawn in part from that writing. But a lot has transpired in my life over the last 30 years. The most significant change is that my wife, Dottie, and I have raised a family. We have watched with joy and enthusiasm as each of our children has matured into a godly adult. All have now left home and married. Some are even providing us with the thrill of grandchildren. And it's additionally rewarding to lock arms in ministry with my son, Sean, as we speak together or write a book together.

What I have discovered since writing that book on understanding the Bible is how much more relevant God's Word is to my life now—especially to my family life. Let me explain what I mean.

I have always believed the truths of the Bible were to be applied to my life. Application is about embracing scriptural truth and adjusting our life to bring it in line with that truth. For example, I may know and believe in my head that God's Word says to forgive others. But application is about actually following through and forgiving people who offend me.

Application of biblical truth is a key component to spiritual growth, but we still need to take one more step beyond application: *making Scripture experientially real.* We need to learn how Scripture is to be lived out in our relationships with God and others. Yes, we need to apply God's commands and be kind, care for others, be honest, faithful, pure, merciful, humble, patient, forgiving others, and so on. Yet God also wants us to experience the receiving and giving of his truth. He wants us to literally experience things like acceptance (Romans 15:7), encouragement (1 Thessalonians 5:11), support (Galatians 6:2), respect (1 Peter 2:17), approval (Romans 14:18), joy (Romans 12:15a), comfort (2 Corinthians 1:3-4), and so on. God wants us to apply his truth to our lives plus experience that truth with him and others. Let me give you an example of what I mean.

Some years ago Dottie came home from a meeting at school very hurt over what some mother had said about one of our kids. In the past when she had shared a problem like that with me, I would evaluate the situation and come up with a scriptural "how shall we then live?" solution. I would say something like, "Well, honey, don't let it get to you. You've got to be patient with people and try not to get too upset with them or resent them." In fact, in this case I could have quoted her Peter's words where he says, "Don't repay evil for evil. Don't retaliate when people say unkind things about you [or your kids]. Instead, pay them back with a blessing. That is what God wants you to do, and he will bless you for it" (1 Peter 3:9 NLT).

---

Dottie needed someone to experience the truth of
Romans 12:15 with her: "When others are happy, be happy
with them. If they are sad, share in their sorrow" (TLB).

---

At other times I would wax theological and offer scriptural insights such as, "Vengeance is mine" or "the LORD will vindicate his people"

(Deuteronomy 32:35 and 36). If Dottie could firm up her belief in God as the One who would judge this critical and unfair person, she would surely feel better. After all, God would be pleased if she would apply this truth to her life.

But on this particular occasion I realized that Dottie was in pain and she needed to experience the comfort of a Scripture passage. At that moment she didn't need to hear a passage on who God is or even how to apply truth to her life. She needed someone to experience the truth of Romans 12:15 with her: "When others are happy, be happy with them. If they are sad, share in their sorrow" (TLB).

So I simply put my arms around her and said, "Honey, I'm so sorry that you had to hear those words, and I hurt for you." That was it—no theology or do this or do that. No plan for dealing with the wrong, but just a heartfelt expression that relationally identified with her pain. And amazingly, it worked. Dottie felt understood and was comforted, and that was all she needed at the moment. A few days later she came back to me and asked what I thought she could do to address those critical comments about our child. My scriptural "application" plan was then welcomed.

Over the years God has led both my dad and me (Sean) on a journey not only to study and apply scriptural truth to our lives, but also to experience loving God more intimately and loving those around us more deeply by experiencing his truth together. My mother felt loved that day when Dad experienced a simple but profound truth with her from God's book. He also felt a deeper sense of love and meaning from "the God of all comfort," who smiled upon his children experiencing the truth of his Word. (See 2 Corinthians 1:3-7.)

Through my father's influence, I have been greatly motivated to become a student of God's Word. I have wanted to know what it says and what it means. But I have been even more blessed for having the privilege of observing firsthand living models of a father and mother who experience God's truth before me and my sisters day in and day out. They weren't perfect models—none of us is—but they were true models of parents who loved God, one another, and their kids. And

I am honored to co-author this book with my dad and relate how together we have gone, and continue to go, beyond mere study to experiencing the Bible.

✑

**In the first part** of this book we will walk you through various ways you can experience the relevance of God's truth to your life. We will lead you to discover the often forgotten purpose of Scripture: how the Word opens the eyes of our hearts; ways to experience Scripture with Jesus and others; and how to ask the right question. We will share examples from our own lives showing how God has taught us to know him and his ways in an intimate, experiential way.

Many of the experiential tools we share here have been greatly influenced by our friend Dr. David Ferguson and his work with the Great Commandment Network. David has spent the major part of his life helping and encouraging those of us in Christian work, especially focusing us on how to experience the Bible in relationship with God and one another. We are deeply indebted to David for both his insights and his help in our own lives and want to acknowledge his contribution to this work. In fact, many of the insights in this first part are drawn from David's teaching seminar "Relational Foundations" and are published in the workbook of the same name.

**In the second part** we will offer tools for probing more deeply into the Scriptures. Here you will be encouraged to examine Scripture passages and experience those truths yourself. We will explore how to interpret the intended meaning of Scripture and explain the tools needed to discover it. We will examine the questions to ask of a passage in order to see the big picture of Scripture and your place in it. And we will offer exercises that will help to clarify the unclear.

Studying God's Word is important. It is the process of searching out the hidden treasures God wants us to discover. But what is most important is that study sets you on a journey toward loving more deeply and becoming more devoted to the author of the Book—God himself. Let the journey begin.

# PART ONE

# Ways the Bible Is Experienced

# Chapter 2

# The Forgotten Purpose of Scripture

The blast of the horn pierced their ears. The ground shook violently. Smoke billowed from the mountain as if it were a volcano. And in that moment a thunderous voice boomed forth—it was the voice of God.

This was a monumental moment in the history of the human race. For the first time since God walked in the Garden with the first couple, he was speaking to his people in an audible voice. But he did more than speak verbally to the children of Israel from Mount Sinai just over three millennia ago. He personally gave Moses "two stone tablets inscribed with the terms of the covenant, written by the finger of God" (Exodus 31:18). "Search all of history," Moses wrote, "from the time God created people on the earth until now…Has anything as great as this ever been seen or heard before?" (Deuteronomy 4:32).

The Almighty God of the universe spoke aloud for all to hear and then personally wrote his words for all to read. Why? What was so important that he chose to reveal himself in such a demonstrative fashion? It was obviously important to him that he be understood clearly, so important that he delivered his message personally. But what was the purpose of speaking and writing his words?

## WHAT IS THE PURPOSE OF THE BIBLE?

The reality is, the eternal, all-powerful Creator of the universe took time to personally write and superintend the writing of a set of documents just for you and for all of us. And whenever God steps out of his eternal day to write something, it's a big deal—it's important. So what is it that he wants us to know, and why does he want us to know it? This is crucial, because if we don't understand the purpose for God's words, we can miss the very meaning and relevance of Scripture to our lives.

Some people say the Bible is a handbook of the Christian religion. Its purpose is to lay out a set of rules and teachings that establish that religion. Others say it tells us how to get to heaven and provides a roadmap on how to get there. But the truth is, most people don't have a clear and comprehensive answer for why God gave us his Book, what story it tells, or what that story has to do with them. Scripture itself, however, gives us that answer.

## A Doctrinal Purpose

They were puzzled. The Pharisees and Sadducees were scholars in religious law, and they were not used to being challenged. But this young rabbi was gathering quite a following, and it had reached the point that he was upstaging them. So they set out to trap him into saying something that would make him look bad in front of the crowds.

---

God's Word...gives us rational truths that we
can understand with our minds. These truths are
doctrinal beliefs that make up our theology.

---

The Sadducees posed a theological question to him about the resurrection, a doctrine they didn't believe in. Jesus answered, "Haven't you ever read about this in the Scriptures? Long after Abraham, Isaac, and Jacob had died, God said, 'I am the God of Abraham, the God of Isaac, and the God of Jacob.' So he is the God of the living, not the dead" (Matthew 22:31-32).

In this incident Jesus quoted Exodus 3:6 with a clear purpose in mind. He wanted to point out that God's Word informs us about what to believe—in this case, what to believe about the doctrine of the resurrection of the dead. Another example: We are taught throughout the New Testament that those who believe that Jesus is the Christ—the Son of God—and place their faith in him shall have eternal life. Jesus said, "I am the resurrection and the life. Those who believe in me, even though they die like everyone else, will live again" (John 11:25 NLT). Scriptures like this informs us as to what we should believe. They are our authority for determining correct doctrine. These passages show that there is a *doctrinal purpose for God's Word*. It gives us rational truths that we can understand with our minds. These truths are doctrinal beliefs that make up our theology.

Many people shy away from the idea of theology. Yet theology is actually the study of God. So in a sense, we are all "theologians." We all have ideas about who God is and what he is like, yet we rarely think of that as knowing "theology." But one of the clear purposes of Scripture is unabashedly theological—to reveal God for who he is. He wants us to know what he is like, how his ways differ from ours, and how he sees life in contrast to how we see it.

The problem is that a large and growing number of adults, especially young adults, in the United States are becoming theologically illiterate. Stephen Prothero states in his book *Religious Literacy: What Every American Needs to Know—And Doesn't* that the Bible instructs us to "'search the Scriptures'…but little searching, and even less finding is being done. "He reports that less than half of Americans can name the first book of the Bible and more than 10 percent think that Joan of Arc was the wife of Noah."[1]

According to a recent Barna Group study most people regard Easter as a religious holiday, but only a minority even associate it with the resurrection of Christ. The findings reveal that a growing majority believes the Holy Spirit is simply a symbol of God's presence and not the third person of the Trinity. And only a few adults actually believe that their faith is to be integrated into every aspect of their existence. In other words, most Americans don't think their belief in God is meant to be the focal point of their lives.[2]

Doctrine does matter. By understanding what the Scriptures reveal about God, for example, we actually understand what he reveals about us. When we see all of life through God's eyes we gain what is called a biblical worldview—a correct view about reality that tells us how the world came to be, who we are as human beings, how to know right from wrong, and so on. These doctrinal truths of Scripture act as boundaries that keep us aligned with correct beliefs so we can see life as God wants us to see it.

One of the keys to the success of the early church in passing on the faith from one generation to another was their clear enunciation of doctrine. They instilled into their children the key truths about God's existence, Scripture, original sin, Christ's atonement, justification through faith, a transformed life, Christ's resurrection, the Trinity, the church, God's kingdom, and Christ's second coming. Check out the Nicene Creed, which was crafted in AD 325 by 300 church leaders to clearly define the Christian faith. You will note that all 12 of the truths we just identified are listed there. (See the creed in its entirety at the end of this chapter.) These doctrinal truths enabled followers of Christ to distinguish the true faith from heresy and cultic spinoffs. They assure us today that God did in fact give "his unchanging truth once for all time to his holy people" (Jude 3) and provided clear guidelines to what we should believe.

Another thing a cohesive, biblical doctrine did for the early church and does for us today is bind us together in unity. The apostle Paul wrote to the church at Colossae, telling them to "put on love, which is the perfect bond of unity" (Colossians 3:14 NASB). He went on to explain that the prerequisite for that unity is letting "the word of Christ richly dwell within you, with all wisdom teaching and admonishing one another" (Colossians 3:16 NASB). Making the Word of God central to our lives and worship brings unity to God's community of believers.

It is important to remember that it is God and his truth that brings unity. He is the one who binds us together, and if we fail to hold to him and his truth we will not experience true unity. That is why Jesus said, "Beware of false prophets who come disguised as harmless sheep, but are really wolves that will tear you apart" (Matthew 7:15 NLT). So rejecting unsound doctrine and distancing ourselves from heretical teaching is not a violation of unity—it is in fact the very course of action that will assure the unity of the church.

Knowing the doctrine of Scripture will not only preserve the unity of God's people, it will also define our values. The Bible teaches us what to believe about God and the world around us, and that belief determines the values we should hold in life. Our beliefs shape what is important and valuable to us. If we have correct beliefs informed by Scripture about God, ourselves, and life, we will have a biblical value system(see diagram).

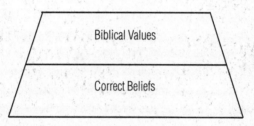

For example, if a person believes that stealing is wrong, he or she will naturally embrace the value that individual ownership of property is to be respected. If a person believes that murder is wrong he or she will naturally embrace the value that human life is sacred. What we believe becomes the basis of our value system. So one purpose of God's Word is to instill correct beliefs into us so that we will embrace a biblical value system.

## A Behavioral Purpose

The Pharisees were masters of the law. They thought that the Scripture provided a checklist of dos and don'ts. One day they tried to trap Jesus with a tax question: "Is it right to pay taxes to Caesar or not?" Jesus answered, "'Here, show me the coin used for the tax.' When they handed him a Roman coin, he asked, 'Whose picture and title are stamped on it?' 'Caesar's,' they replied. 'Well, then,' he said, 'give to Caesar what belongs to Caesar, and give to God what belongs to God'" (Matthew 22:17-21).

The Pharisees were asking a politically charged question. But Jesus simply reinforced the scriptural teaching about our relationship to governing authorities: We are to give obedience to those who are due obedience. The Bible is full of such teaching in the form of laws, commandments, and instructions for living. That is why we can say there is a *behavioral purpose for God's Word.* When the Bible says, "Follow this way," "Avoid those places," "Abstain from those actions," or "Embrace those thoughts," it is instruction in how to live rightly.

God's laws and instructions act as a boundary to tell us what is right and wrong and that living out God's ways is in our best interest. As Moses told the nation of Israel, "Obey the LORD's commands and decrees that I am giving you today for your own good" (Deuteronomy 10:13). Obeying God's Word is always in our long-term best interest. It directs us down the correct path of living. Wise Solomon said it is God who "guards the paths of justice and protects those who are faithful to him. Then you will understand what is right, just, and fair, and you will know how to find the right course of action every time" (Proverbs 2:8-9 NLT). Correct beliefs shape our values and our values drive right actions (see diagram).

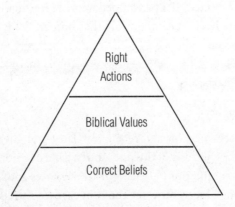

You have probably read the studies that show when people, especially young people, lack a basic biblical belief system they are two or three times more likely to steal, become violent, use illegal drugs, be resentful, and lack purpose in life. Why? Because 1) doctrinal truths of the Bible provide a correct view of God and his ways; and 2) when we embrace his thinking and live accordingly, we reap the benefits of godliness. On the other hand, harboring incorrect beliefs about God and his ways distorts our values, making it unlikely that our actions will be right. The natural fallout will be that we suffer the consequences of wrong living. "The LORD grants wisdom! From his mouth come knowledge and understanding. He grants a treasure of good sense to the godly. He is their shield, protecting those who walk with integrity" (Proverbs 2:7-8 NLT). So another reason God gave us his Word is so we can live out his truth correctly. The doctrines and commands of Scripture then act as two guardrails that guide us down a path of righteousness.

## Is Something Missing?

Paul made it clear to Timothy that God gave us his Word for a doctrinal and behavioral purpose: "All Scripture is inspired by God and profitable for teaching, for reproof, for correction" (2 Timothy 3:16 NASB). The English phrase "inspired by God" is translated from the Greek *theopneustos*, which means "God-breathed." The word rendered "teaching" in this passage is the Greek word *didaskalia*, which means "doctrine," or "correct teaching." Paul is telling us that God gave us his Word so we can believe rightly.

Paul also says here that God gave us his Word to provide reproof and correction. So we can say that the Bible is his way of correcting us when we're wrong and restoring us to living rightly.

This is all scripturally correct and vitally important. But do you sense that something is still missing? The Pharisees and religious leaders in Jesus' time got this much right, but Jesus had harsh words for them and their religiosity. They taught the importance of the law and knew all the doctrines. Yet their higher learning and educational degrees seemed to prompt arrogance. They minutely defined the commandments of Scripture and dutifully performed them to the letter. Yet their legalistic behavior seemed to prompt an attitude of judgmentalism. What was missing from their understanding of Scripture?

The answer lies in Jesus' answer to a question posed by an expert in religious law: "'Which is the most important commandment in the law of Moses?' Jesus replied, 'You must love the LORD your God with all your heart, all your soul, and all your mind.' This is the first and greatest commandment. A second is equally important: 'Love your neighbor as yourself'" (Matthew 22:36-39).

---

> Was Jesus implying that Scripture was given to lead
> us into a deepened relationship with the One who
> wrote the Book—and then with those around us?

---

Jesus first quotes from Deuteronomy 6:5, which was part of the Shema—used by these religious leaders every day: "The LORD is our God, the LORD is one!" (Deuteronomy 6:4 NASB). Then he combines the commandment to love God found in Deuteronomy 6 with a command from Leviticus 19:18 to love your neighbor as yourself.

Jesus was telling this Pharisee that the greatest, most important commandments were to love God with everything he had and love his neighbors as he loved himself. But Jesus didn't stop there. He followed up with a most profound statement: "The entire law and all the demands of the prophets are based on these two commandments" (Matthew 22:40). He was apparently saying that all doctrinal teaching and instructions for living hang on one great commandment to love God and one another. Was he implying that Scripture was given to lead us into a deepened relationship with the One who wrote the Book— and then with those around us? If so, such a concept would have a profound effect on the way we understand the truths of the Bible.

## A Relational Purpose

The Pharisees and other religious leaders had seemingly grasped the doctrinal and behavioral purposes of Scripture. What they failed to understand was the connection of right beliefs and right behavior to the Great Commandment.

Of course, the Hebrew Scriptures were filled with the connection between truth and relationships, but the Pharisees had obviously missed them. King David said in his Psalm, "I am always aware of your unfailing love, and I have lived according to your truth" (Psalm 26:3). Then he prayed, "Teach me your ways, O LORD, that I may live according to your truth!" (Psalm 86:11). The Old Testament writers understood truth within the context of relationships. Jesus' declaration was simply a reframing of doctrinal beliefs and obedience, restoring them to their rightful place within the context of relationship, which had been lost by the religionists of his day. He was proclaiming that there was a *relational purpose for God's Word*. These religious leaders had failed to place their right thinking and right living in the context of right relationship. Consequently, this severely distorted their thinking and living.

The truth is, we simply cannot get our doctrinal thinking correct, no matter how many theological degrees we earn, unless we see those doctrinal truths through the lens of right relationship. We cannot even get our adherence to biblical commands right without living them out within the context of right relationship. All biblical doctrines and scriptural commands, Jesus said, are "based on [hang on] these two commandments" of relationship with God and relationship with others.

Just how does the relational purpose of God's Word change the way we read and study Scripture, believe its doctrinal truths, and obey its biblical commands? That's the question we'll unpackage next.

## RELATIONSHIPS AS THE FOUNDATION

Long before rain fell from the sky, before rivers flowed from the mountains to the seas, before there were humans or animal life, before the sun, moon, and stars were ever created, before angels existed... there was relationship. God was all that existed, but he did not exist in a void or a vacuum. He was not suspended in a universe of nothingness. He did not anguish in cosmic aloneness. Where God was and is and always will be, infinite love exists in perfect relationship.

God, consisting as he does of three Persons within the Trinity, shows us that intimate relationship has existed eternally. He didn't create angelic beings or humans because he needed a relationship; he already had relationship. He exists as relationship. The Father has always infinitely loved the Son. The Son has always infinitely loved the Father. The Holy Spirit has always infinitely loved both the Father and the Son. A continuous cycle of perfect relationships is eternally being experienced within the Godhead. While we can barely begin to comprehend such a perfect and continuing relationship, it is something we all long to experience. That is because we were created in the relational image and likeness of God himself (see Genesis 1:26).

In our human relationships we try to share in the joy and pain of those we love, yet we do that imperfectly. We try to anticipate and meet the needs of our children, yet we do that imperfectly. We try and understand the dreams and expectations of our spouse, yet we do that imperfectly. We love imperfectly because God's image and likeness upon us have been blemished by sin, which has separated us from him. Even though we may be redeemed and reconciled to him through Christ, we have much to learn about the depth and breadth of this experience called relationship. The encouraging thing is that God wants to lead us into a deepened, continuous, and growing relationship as it was meant to be experienced in the beginning. That is why he has spoken to us and given us his Word.

It's true, as we stated before, that beliefs shape our values and values drive our actions. Yet the reality is that we interpret what we believe about God, ourselves, and all of life through our past experiences and relationships—whether those experiences and relationships were healthy or unhealthy.

All that we have learned and everything we know, even *how* we learned it, comes out of a relationship with someone or something. We don't often think of it this way, but much of what we are today is a direct result of who we're related to and how. And it is out of these relationships that we establish our beliefs. Relationships are the fertile ground in which our beliefs grow that shape our values that drive our actions (see diagram).

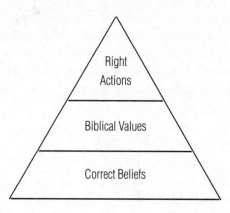

God's ultimate intention for all humanity from creation forward was for every person to enjoy the perfect circle of loving relationship that he enjoyed within the Godhead. He wanted to disclose himself to humans so they could know him for who he is. This is the ultimate *doctrinal truth* that God intended for humans and the universe. He also wanted his creation to live within the boundaries of his ways, which was the only way they could enjoy all the goodness of a perfect world. This is the ultimate *behavioral truth* that he intended for us. God's intent was that the first couple, Adam and Eve, would believe that he is perfectly good and that when he gave them a command, he had their best interest at heart. His intent was that they would understand that he wanted them to love him dearly, and that his one command was given within the context of this *relational truth*.

But they did not. And unfortunately, humans have been missing God's relational context ever since. But the day Jesus answered the Pharisees' question about the greatest commandment stands out in history—the Lord of the universe was reframing all the doctrinal and behavioral truths of Scripture. By distilling everything to "Love God and love each other," he was showing us the dual boundaries of *what we are to believe* and *how we are to behave* within the *loving context of deepened relationship with him*.

Many of us, however, were not taught the relational side of truth. Dr. David Ferguson of the Great Commandment Network explains,

Many of us get sidetracked on this journey toward a deep, intimate relationship with God. We carefully look to Scripture in order to tell us what to believe and how we should behave, but we end up simply veering to one side or the other and miss the opportunity to more deeply know the God of the Bible.[3]

## THE RELATIONAL GOD OF THE BIBLE

The Bible reveals a personal God, the God who "would speak to Moses face to face, as one speaks to a friend" (Exodus 33:11). It is the revelation of "a God who is passionate about his relationship with you" (Exodus 34:14 NLT). And it is a revelation that, from the first words Moses penned in the book of Genesis to the last word John wrote in Revelation, reflects the loving heart of a God who wants us to know him intimately so we can enjoy all the benefits that relationship offers.

---

The Bible reveals an infinite God who is holy,
all-powerful, and all-knowing—and yet personal—
who considers us so valuable he longs to relate to us.

---

Moses understood this, of course. He begged God, "If you are pleased with me, teach me your ways *so I may know you*" (Exodus 33:13 NIV). Jesus prayed to his Father, "This is the way to have eternal life—to know you, the only true God, and Jesus Christ, the one you sent to earth" (John 17:3). God spoke through Hosea the prophet, who said, "Oh that we might know the LORD! Let us press on to know him…I want you to show love, not offer sacrifices. I want you to know me" (Hosea 6:3,6).

What does it do to your heart to know that the mighty God of the universe is so relational that he makes himself vulnerable enough to say, "I want you to know me"? You might question this astounding fact and say, "It's hard to believe that the infinite and all-sufficient God, who is not limited by time, space, humanity, or anything else, would desire that I know him deeply." But the reality is this: The infinite God is also personal. And because he is personal we can love him, worship him, and please him with our trust and obedience. Because he is personal he can love us, rejoice with us, comfort us, and reveal himself and his ways to us.

In contrast, the gods of ancient Greek and Roman mythology were so "personal" that they were finite—having weaknesses, frequent moral failures, and even petty jealousies. Deism portrays yet another kind of god—one so infinite that he coldly removes himself from the world and shuns involvement in it. Pantheism contends that God is infinitely everywhere and is composed of everything, making him (or it) too cosmic and diffuse to relate to us personally.

The Bible, however, reveals an infinite God who is holy, all-powerful, and all-knowing—and yet personal—who considers us so valuable he longs to relate to us. That is the nature of relationship; it is about wanting to connect intimately with and know another. It is as though God is saying, "I want you to open up to me and invite me into your life so I can experience every aspect of your life with you. And while I am omniscient and therefore know all there is to know about you, I want you to reveal yourself fully to me. In turn, I will step-by-step reveal myself to you. I want you to know me for who I am." As hard as it may be to comprehend, your infinite, personal God has given you his Spirit and the Word so you can learn and love and live in an intimate relationship with him. He does this because he wants to be one with you.

## THE PURPOSE OF THE BIBLE

God offers to give of himself to us, and he longs for us to give ourselves wholly to him as a child gives herself to a loving father. Let's consider again what Paul wrote to Timothy about the purpose of Scripture: "All Scripture is inspired by God and profitable for teaching, for reproof, for correction" (2 Timothy 3:16 NASB). This passage tells us that Scripture is not only profitable for teaching (right doctrine) and for reproof and correction (right behavior), it goes on to add a third purpose: "for training in righteousness."

The word "training" is translated from the Greek word *paideia*—to "bring up," as in to "raise" or "parent" a child. This passage suggests that God's Word is designed to "parent" us.

But how? How can a set of words in a book raise us? Parenting is a person-to-person function. Yet Jesus does explain how the Word of God in fact does that. He said, "I will ask the Father, and he will give you another Counselor, who will never leave you. He is the Holy Spirit, who leads into all truth" (John 14:16-17 NLT). It is God the Father who has sent his Holy Spirit to "parent" us. The Holy Spirit comes to show us God himself and his truth in the words he has written. He helps us understand who God wants us to be and how he wants us to love and live.

If, as Paul said, Scripture was given to raise us, why do we need the "parenting" of the Holy Spirit? Think of it this way: What is it that really "parents" our children properly? Is it the directives, instructions, and commands that we give them? Those are "behavioral guidelines," but they are not what raises our kids. It is *parents*—relational human beings—who raise our children. That is the way God designed it. He wants kids to be brought up through loving relationships. Without relationship, all attempts to instill values, beliefs, and right behaviors will be ineffective because they are detached from the necessary elements of personal love and care. Truth without relationships leads to rejection, and discipline or correction without relationship leads to anger and resentment. But when you place truth within the context of a loving relationship, you almost always get a positive response.

The Holy Spirit administers Scripture to us like a loving parent in order to provide us with wisdom through its lessons (Proverbs 3:5), security through its boundaries (Exodus 20), caution through its warnings (Ephesians 4:17-22), and reproof through its discipline (Philippians 2:3-4). We may study God's Word for correct beliefs. We may even obey God's Word for right behavior. But we must not forget why. The relational God of the Bible wants us to relationally experience his love and the love of those around us. We can then say that *God gave us the Bible because he wants an intimate loving relationship with us, wants us to enjoy intimate loving relationships with one another, and wants our relationships together to extend us and his kingdom into eternity.*

To reinforce God's desire for restored relationship in your own heart, read and meditate on the following words of Jesus from the book of John. Let them sink deep into your heart. Your God longs for you to know him intimately. He longs to fulfill you, complete you, and give you joy as you love him and one another. That is why he has given you his Spirit and his Word.

"You search the Scriptures because you think they give you eternal life. But the Scriptures point to me!" (John 5:39). "My purpose is to give life in all its fullness" (John 10:10 NLT). "I have told you this so that my joy may be in you and that your joy may be complete. My commandment is this: Love each other as I have loved you" (John 15:11-12 NIV). "My prayer for all of them is that they will be one, just as you and I are one, Father—that just as you are in me and I am in you, so they will be in us, and the world will believe you sent me" (John 17:21 NLT).

Does reading Jesus' words prompt you to think of Scripture differently than you have in the past? Does it change the way you see doctrinal truth or give you a new reason to obey biblical commands? As a young Christian I (Josh) read and studied the Bible. At first, I did it to understand what I should believe and how I should live. But over time those who were discipling me helped me to see the "why" behind my believing and behaving. As I began to see God's heart—his motives, his plans, and his purpose for my life—it changed everything. My personal relationships changed. I began to learn how to take relationships to a deeper level. My sense of purpose and meaning in the world came into focus. I reordered my priorities. Life became an adventure. I embraced a whole new set of plans and goals in life that were exciting and fulfilling.

In short, seeing and reading and living the Scriptures within the context of relationship made life worth living in ways I never thought possible. It didn't come easily or naturally. It was a process and an approach that resulted in a new method of studying and experiencing his Word. Over the years I have tried to pass this approach and method on to my children. And now my son, Sean, joins me in sharing with you in the following chapters how experiencing God's Word can literally revolutionize your life. Read on.

### THE NICENE CREED

We believe in one God, the Father Almighty, Maker of heaven and earth, and of all things visible and invisible;

And in one Lord Jesus Christ, the only begotten Son of God, begotten of his Father before all worlds, God of God, Light of Light, very God of very God, begotten, not made, being of one substance with the Father; by whom all things were made; who for us men and for our salvation came down from heaven, and was incarnate by the Holy Spirit of the Virgin Mary, and was made man; and was crucified also for us under Pontius Pilate; he suffered and was buried; and the third day he rose again according to the Scriptures, and ascended into heaven, and is seated at the right hand of the Father; and he shall come again, with glory, to judge both the living and the dead; whose kingdom shall have no end.

And we believe in the Holy Ghost, the Lord and giver of life, who proceeds from the Father and the Son; who with the Father and the Son together is worshipped and glorified; who spoke by the prophets. And we believe in the holy catholic and apostolic church; we acknowledge one baptism for the remission of sins; and look for the resurrection of the dead, and the life of the world to come.[4]

Chapter 3

# Opening the Eyes of Our Hearts

Scott became a Christian while in college, but he consistently lived under a dark cloud of guilt over his past sins. As a teenager, he was involved in sexual immorality. After he trusted Christ, he changed his lifestyle because he knew immorality was wrong according to Scripture. But he could not escape the sense that God still condemned him for his past sin. He felt like a second-class Christian; he felt that God would never trust him with anything important to do because of his teenage promiscuity. As a result he felt defeated most of the time.

Scott knew in his mind that God had forgiven him. He had read Romans 8:1: "There is no condemnation for those who belong to Christ Jesus." But his lingering false sense of guilt distorted his view of God's grace and kept him trapped in a cycle of self-condemnation. Many of us read the Bible through a distorted lens of past experiences. Things we have done or relationships we have had, especially with family members, play a critical role in shaping our view of ourselves and our life.

Medical research has established that we are biologically "hardwired" to connect with others—starting, of course, with our parents. The research has led to the development of what is known as *attachment theory*. The concept behind this theory is that we were born with the need to make secure attachments with others. We will inevitably make attachments, and if we can't make secure attachments, we make insecure ones—even if they negatively affect our lives.

Mark Matlock, president of WisdomWorks Ministries, wrote about the attachment theory in my (Sean's) book *Apologetics for a New Generation*. He said,

> Dr. Todd Hall at Rosemead School of Psychology has done some interesting work applying the attachment theory to our relationship with God. If insecure human attachments keep us from healthy connections with others, couldn't they keep us from connecting with God as well?[1]

Experience has shown that to be the case—our perception of God is colored by our child-parent relationship, especially the relationship with a father.

---

How you related to your parents and they with you has no doubt greatly influenced your perception of God.

---

Many people have wondered why our current generation is falling away from the faith and not embracing the values of their families. In his book *Faith of the Fatherless: The Psychology of Atheism*, psychologist Paul Vitz shows that the great atheists of the past almost without exception had distant, dead, or harsh fathers. He calls this "the theory of the defective father."[2] According to Vitz, once a child loses respect for his or her earthly father, then belief in a heavenly father is greatly impaired. Vitz supports his case by pointing to the lives of prominent atheists such as Sigmund Freud, Jean-Paul Sartre, Karl Marx, Bertrand Russell, Madalyn Murray O'Hair, Friedrich Nietzsche, and many more. Vitz does not present these examples as arguments for theism. Rather, he simply shows how psychological factors, especially the relationship with the father, influence our view about God.

So how you related to your parents and they with you has no doubt greatly influenced your perception of God. For example, if you grew up with authoritarian parents and felt their disapproval or felt relationally distant from them, you will likely tend to project those feelings into your relationship with God. You will naturally bring that distorted lens to your reading of Scripture, causing you to see him as an authoritarian, disapproving figure.

## WHAT KIND OF GOD DO YOU SEE?

During the Passover meal, often referred to as the Last Supper, Jesus shared many things with his disciples. One of those things is found in John 14, when Jesus said, "If you love Me, you will keep My commandments" (John 14:15 NASB).

Now imagine yourself seated across the table from Jesus there in the upper room. He looks your way, and you make eye contact with the Master as he says, "If you love me, you will keep my commandments." What would be your response to his statement? What would go on in your mind as to the reason he would be saying these words to you?

### Is Jesus Disappointed?

A person like Scott would probably hear Jesus' words through his feelings of false guilt. In his mind's eye he would see Jesus crossing his arms and shaking his head saying, "If you really loved me you would have kept my commandments all along. Your failings before and even now speak volumes. Scott, you are such a disappointment to me."

What do *you* hear in Jesus' voice as he makes his statement about love and commandments? If you sense his disappointment as Scott does, you might compensate by working harder at performing for God in hopes of feeling worthy of his love. Problem is, none of us can live the Christian life perfectly. If we sense a disappointed God in Scripture we will tend to see his love as a meritorious reward for good performance. This will often cause us to see only the "thou shalt nots" of the Bible and miss its many promises. This view sets up our emotions to feel, *I must do right to be loved right.* And invariably this perception will permeate all our relationships.

Performance-driven people sometimes tend to use their own fear of being a disappointment as a form of coercion to motivate others. They expect from others the same kind of performance they demand of themselves, and when others fail to give it, they communicate to those others the same disappointment they feel hovering over them.

As a result, friends and family begin to feel that "nothing is ever good enough for him or her." This behavior does nothing but perpetuate the misconception that loving someone is intrinsically attached to how he or she performs.

## Is Jesus Inspecting Us?

When Jesus says, "*If* you love me you will keep my commandments" do you see him raising his eyebrows and stressing the first word? Do you hear a questioning tone in his voice as if his statement is really something of a warning: "Do you know that I'm watching you to see if you keep my commandments?"

Some see God in just this way—as an inspector who is grading us on how well we follow the directives in the Bible. Is that the kind of God you see? One who stands over you with a pad and pencil, keeping a running tally of all your deeds, both good and bad? Like a celestial Santa Claus he's "making a list, checking it twice, gonna find out who's naughty or nice." It's hard to imagine a God such as this celebrating who you are or being happy to commune with you in prayer. His scrutinizing, inspecting eye would sap the joy out of the relationship.

If we see God as such an inspector we might tend to take even the slightest corrective suggestion from others as a personal attack and become defensive. We may also be prone to take on the role of inspector ourselves and suspiciously monitor the behavior of others. We might make big deals out of minor biblical issues. As you can imagine, people find it difficult to enjoy the fellowship of someone who keeps them under scrutiny and records any deviation from the letter of the law.

## Is Jesus Distant?

Do you see Jesus raising his hand somewhat absentmindedly with his head down and in an indifferent voice say something like, "Oh, by the way, if you love me you might think about keeping some of my commandments and stuff…whatever." This kind of God might have time to talk to only the "important people" who are doing the "important things" in life. And you probably don't qualify.

Many people, especially today's young people, have experienced absentee parents. Mom and Dad were somewhere in their growing-up years but not caringly involved in their lives. And consequently they project this distant parental relationship on their relationship with God. David Ferguson shares his and his wife's early concept of God.

> For many years I struggled with a god who inspected and was often disappointed in my life. My wife, Theresa, came to view God as distant. She noted one day that "it was hard for me to imagine that God even noticed when I woke up in the morning. I was never convinced that he truly knew me or cared what was important to me. I saw God as some-one who only had time for the 'big stuff' of this world, and I certainly wasn't included. This distant god was hard to get to know or trust, and seemed disinterested in know-ing me."[3]

This distant view of God will affect what we believe he has in store for us. His promises would obviously not be for us. He is powerful, but his power wouldn't be available to us. A distant God has little relevance to our lives.

## OPENING OUR EYES TO THE REAL GOD

Back when I (Sean) was in college a few Christian friends invited me to their Bible study group. As a single college student I wanted to develop the discipline of getting into God's Word with my fellow class-mates. But what struck me was the lens through which a couple of my buddies read practically every verse. They always seemed to have at least three questions they had to ask about each passage:

1. What sin here needs to be avoided? (*Because an inspecting God is watching.*)

2. What commandment here needs to be obeyed? (*Because an inspecting God is keeping track.*)

3. What part of my life needs to be changed? (*Because a disappointed God requires perfect performance.*)

It is not that we shouldn't avoid sin or understand what biblical commands we need to obey. But when we view God's Word through the lens of a disappointed, inspecting, or distant God we distort his truth. Paul prayed for the Christ-followers in Ephesus. He prayed that God would "give you the Spirit of wisdom and revelation, so that you may know [Jesus] better…that the eyes of your heart may be enlightened in order that you may know the hope to which he has called you" (Ephesians 1:17-18 NIV).

In verse 17 of this passage, the word for "wisdom" in the Greek is *ophia*, which is wisdom in spiritual truth providing insight into the true nature of things. The word "revelation" in the Greek is *apokalupsis*, meaning the uncovering or unveiling of the knowledge of God to the soul. In other words, when Paul prayed that the eyes of our hearts might be enlightened, he was asking God to peel back the distorted view we have of him and let us see the true nature of who Jesus is until it penetrates deep into our inner soul.

We can truly approach Scripture with this heartfelt prayer. God wants to open the eyes of our hearts to see him, the real God, for who he is. He wants to disabuse our minds and emotions of seeing a disappointed, inspecting, or distant God brought about by past or present unhealthy relationships. He wants his holy Word to purify, cleanse, and rectify any distortions we may have of him. And as we do we can experience him, the real God, as he meant us to experience him.

## JESUS AS THE ACCEPTING GOD

Paul said, "Accept each other just as Christ has accepted you; then God will be given glory" (Romans 15:7). This wording indicates that rather than being a disappointed or inspecting or distant God, he is an accepting God. But just how accepting is he?

The word translated "accept" here is the Greek word *proslambano*, or "receive." It doesn't refer to a casual reception of another. It carries with it the sense of receiving another person with a special and deep interest. It is a full embrace without reservations and conditions. It is an open-arms welcome.

To help get a clearer picture of Christlike acceptance let's look at John 4, where Jesus meets the woman at the well. Scripture says Jesus "left Judea to return to Galilee. He had to go through Samaria on the way" (John 4:3-4). Jesus' travel itinerary is the first indicator of how accepting he is.

---

A true follower of Judaism would not dignify the Samaritans— or pollute himself or herself—by even walking on their soil.

---

Reality was, Jesus didn't have to go through Samaria to get to Galilee. The "devoted" Jews of the day would never go through Samaria to get to Galilee from Judea. Galilee was due north of Judea, and Samaria was right in the middle. So a Jewish person would either travel around that region by going east to Jericho then following the Jordan Valley north, or they could travel by boat west of the area via the Mediterranean Sea. Whatever the case, a strict Jewish person would consider the longer journey around well worth it.

Samaria had a long history of tension with Judea. In Jesus' day Jews considered Samaritans "half-breeds." They didn't believe they had the right pedigree (pure bloodline), so they wanted nothing to do with them. Additionally, Samaritans claimed that Mount Gerizim was the proper place to worship, while the Jews insisted that authentic worship could take place only in Jerusalem. In effect, Jews considered Samaritans heretics. So a true follower of Judaism would not dignify the Samaritans—or pollute himself or herself—by even walking on their soil.

Obviously, Jesus' feelings toward the Samaritans were different. He made his journey right through the middle of Samaria until he came to Sychar, "and Jesus, tired from the long walk, sat wearily beside the well [Jacob's well] about noontime" (John 4:6).

This was an arid and dry land. Water was a precious commodity. People would come to this well in the morning before the day heated up or in the cool of the evening. Few would come at noontime. Anyone foolish enough to be gathering water at this time of day probably was trying to avoid being seen by the townspeople.

Jesus was no doubt sitting near the well. He was alone, waiting on his disciples who had gone into town to buy food. Then along came a Samaritan woman to draw water from the well. Not expecting to see anyone, she probably began to draw water and didn't even see Jesus. Startled by the voice behind her she heard a man say, "Please give me a drink" (verse 7).

The woman's response is significant: "You are a Jew, and I am a Samaritan woman. Why are you asking me for a drink?" (verse 9). This woman was shocked on two levels. First, this was a *man* who was talking to her. It was highly unusual for a man to speak to an unfamiliar woman. To do so was considered shameful, illicit and, at times, even scandalous. Notice in verse 27 that when the disciples showed up, "They were shocked to find him talking to a woman." In that day, men with good intentions just didn't talk to women who were strangers.

Secondly, Jewish men or women simply didn't converse with the heretical Samaritans. So it's clear the woman was taken aback by the very fact that he spoke to her. She must have thought, *This is a different kind of man.* Then notice what Jesus says: "If you only knew the gift God has for you and who you are speaking to, you would ask me, and I would give you living water" (verse 10).

Now he really had this woman confused. Not only did this man consider her worth talking to, he offered her an extraordinary gift. She knew the difference between "dead" and "living" water. "Living water" referred to moving water, like a fresh river or spring. "Dead water" was standing or stored water. Samaria had no rivers, so Jesus' statement was confusing. If Jacob had had to dig a well there, how could this man be offering her fresh, superior water?

But naturally, if he could deliver on the fresh water, she was up for it. "Please, sir," the woman said, "give me this water! Then I'll never be thirsty again, and I won't have to come here to get water" (verse 15).

Then the Master throws her a big curve. "'Go and get your husband,' Jesus told her" (verse 16). Of course he knew she had five previous husbands and the man she was now living with wasn't her husband—and he told her that. Recognizing his prophetic skills, she switched the subject to who was worshipping correctly, Jews or Samaritans.

Something must have begun to dawn on her. This man was truly different. He had spoken to a strange woman, which was unusual. He was a Jewish man who spoke to a Samaritan, which was even more unusual. Then he offered to direct her to some unknown fresh water source. And that was truly extraordinary. On top of all of that, he knew more about her than probably a lot of her friends—what few she had left. This led her to inquire about spiritual things like worship and the Messiah.

So she stated her own belief: "'I know the Messiah is coming—the one who is called Christ. When he comes, he will explain everything to us.'" Then Jesus revealed the truth of his relationship to her: "'I am the Messiah!'" (verses 25-26). He was saying, "Yes, I may be a man, and I may be a Jewish man, but I'm really your Messiah, your deliverer, the one you have been longing for." At that point her excitement was more than she could take, and she headed back to the village to spread the news of who she had met.

Let's recap the extraordinarily different way in which this man named Jesus received this woman, and how she must have reasoned:

- *I am a woman and he is a man. And he can see I'm the kind of woman that strange men have no business talking to. Why is he talking to me?*

- *He is a Jew, and Jews despise us Samaritans. What's wrong with him?*

- *I am an adulterer, which makes it near impossible for even a decent man to interact with me, let alone the Holy Messiah. What is going on here?*

This Samaritan woman had never encountered such a man—one who was so receptive, so open to her, so welcoming. She knew Jesus had no cause to accept her the way he did. Being an immoral woman she was rejected by most. She must have felt alienated and alone. But despite all that, this extraordinary Jesus received her with open arms.

His acceptance didn't mean he condoned her adultery; he did not. Yet he didn't show disappointment in who she was either. He still saw the beauty, the potential, and the innate worth and dignity God infused into every human by virtue of creation, and he loved her for it. Nor was he "Jesus the inspector," even though she wasn't worshipping correctly. He was the compassionate corrector, loving her enough to tell her the truth. And he certainly wasn't a distant God, because he was visiting her in her own environment. Jesus' acceptance of her had nothing to do with her own actions. Nothing she could say or do or not say or not do would cause the Messiah to take her in as he did, to show her such respect, and let her know she was so welcome in his presence. He accepted her as she was and gave her a vision of who she could be. That is the nature of the real God.

Now, that isn't to say God simply overlooks our sin and in effect says, "That's okay, everybody messes up. I'll just forget your past sins." The reality is that he by nature is holy. He can't just overlook sin. The Bible says of him, "Your eyes are too pure to look on evil; you cannot tolerate wrong" (Habakkuk 1:13 NIV). God is so holy that he "cannot allow sin in any form" (Habakkuk 1:13 NLT). So what does he do?

Our sin, of course, has resulted in death—separation from God. And we are by no means acceptable to him in our sinful state. Add to that the fact we are unable to do anything to change our sinful and dead status, and it would appear we are doomed forever (see Romans 6:23 and Ephesians 2:1). But our plight is unacceptable to God. Why? Because he loves us and wants to restore us to a relationship with him. So he provides a redemptive plan of salvation.

"God saved you by his special favor when you believed," Paul said. "And you can't take credit for this; it is a gift from God. Salvation is not a reward for the good things we have done, so none of us can boast about it" (Ephesians 2:8-9 NLT). Even though his holiness cannot embrace our life of sin, his heart accepts us without condition. So despite our being sinners, he offers us grace. And it is that grace that cost him the life's blood of his only Son. And because of that holy sacrifice he can welcome us regardless of who we are or what we've done. With open arms he says, "Come to me—I love you and will forgive you, not based on any of your efforts, but because of my Son's atoning sacrifice and resurrection."

When we realize that God knows us for who we ar̶ faults, failures, and sin, it's not easy to grasp that he is so a̶ he is. Bill and Gloria Gaither nailed it when they wrote the song Loved." In it we sing, "The one who knows me best loves me most. The Jesus of the Bible is an accepting God.

## JOHN 14:15 SPOKEN BY AN ACCEPTING JESUS

Now, let's go back to the upper room. You are again seated across from Jesus. Your eyes meet. This is your Savior, who sees you just the way you are and loves and accepts you beyond your wildest dreams. He tells you there are many rooms in his Father's house and he is going to prepare a place for you. Then he makes you a promise—"I will come and get you, so that you will always be with me where I am" (John 14:3).

Jesus now explains that the works he has done were actually not of his own doing: It was the Father working through him. So he makes you another promise—"Anyone who believes in me will do the same works I have done" (John 14:12).

---

Lay aside your preconceived ideas of God based on your past relationships with others and allow Scripture to define the accepting Jesus, who loves you beyond belief.

---

He smiles reassuringly and gives you yet another promise—"You can ask for anything in my name, and I will do it" (John 14:13). None of these promises sound like they are coming from a disappointed or inspecting or distant Jesus, do they? They are coming from a Jesus who welcomes you and receives you with a full embrace without reservations or conditions. Then in a tender voice and with accepting eyes he makes you a final promise. Listen to his words as he extends his arms toward you and with a smile on his face says, "If you love Me, you will keep My commandments" (John 14:15 NASB).

This verse is a very special promise to you. It is meant to bring reassurance, security, and confidence to your heart. Listen to his promise in the next two verses: "And I will ask the Father and he will give you another Counselor, who will never leave you. He is the Holy Spirit, who leads into all truth" (John 14:16-17 NLT). Doesn't this give you incredible confidence? He is in effect saying, "If you and I have a loving relationship, I promise I am not going to leave you alone to try to live the Christian life in your own strength. I'm going to take up residence in your life through the power and person of my Holy Spirit, and I will be there to empower you. Together we will become one—my nature will be your nature, my desires will become your desires, my ways will become your ways."

This is the promise that comes to us from the accepting Jesus. And when we embrace his promise, his love becomes real to us. In fact, it is his transforming love that enables us to love him back so deeply and love each other as he loves us.

Lay aside your preconceived ideas of God based on your past relationships with others and allow Scripture to define the accepting Jesus, who loves you beyond belief. He loves you and every one of us in spite of our sin. And as stated earlier, he has mercifully provided atonement for sin at great cost to himself. He separates who we are from what we have done and loves us for who we are. Then he accepts—receives with welcoming arms—each of us at the point of our failure.

That is the God the Bible reveals—the real God. Receive his unconditional acceptance and experience freedom from false guilt and self-condemnation. Respond to the welcoming embrace of the Savior and rest in his secure arms. Reach out and grasp his promise and be infused with his Holy Spirit, who empowers you to live pleasing to him.

If we are to go beyond mere study of scriptural text and experience God's truth, we must see Jesus for who he is—the real God who loves and accepts us without condition. He is there with outstretched arms, longing to lead us through his Word so we can know him more intimately. Seeing God through a lens other than the loving and accepting Jesus will distort his truth, and that truth will become irrelevant to our lives.

This is a basic prerequisite to correctly interpreting and experiencing God's Word. It is a fundamental truth that must be in place in our lives in order to experience God's book. We must accept the accepting

Jesus. In the next two chapters we will build off this foundation stone—the foundation of an accepting Jesus—which will enable us to experience Scripture passages with God and with one another.

The following quote from David Ferguson brings a fitting close to this chapter:

> The real Christ is attentive and caring, sensitive and compassionate. He does not have a tally sheet in heaven, and is not too preoccupied to care about each of us individually. He is not detached or distant, disappointed or displeased. The real Christ wants to be close, intimate friends with you and me. He is excited when we wake up in the morning, and cannot wait to talk with us. He is delighted to know us and be with us. He is pleased with you because he sees you with the eyes of a Master Creator, one who admires his handiwork and values you as his treasure because you are his very own child.[5]

"May you experience the love of Christ, though it is so great you will never fully understand it. Then you will be filled with the fullness of life and power that comes from God" (Ephesians 3:19 NLT).

Chapter 4

# Experiencing Jesus in Scripture

It is a sunny Sabbath afternoon. Jesus has just exited the temple, where he has been accused by the religious leaders of being possessed by a demon.

Walking briskly away, followed by his disciples, Jesus sees a blind beggar sitting cross-legged on the street, as is typical. We see the Master gazing at the man, who is a fixture in the area because he frequently begs at this spot. Though few know the beggar's name, most know his circumstances; he has been blind since birth.

We turn with the disciples, and tentatively, we approach the pair—the beggar and the Teacher—wondering why Jesus has stopped here. "'Teacher,' his disciples asked him, 'why was this man born blind? Was it a result of his own sin or those of his parents?'" (John 9:2 NLT).

The first issue the disciples want to address about this beggar is his sin. But not Jesus. With characteristic kindness he plants his knees in the dirt beside the man and answers, more to him than to the questioner, "It was not because of his sins or his parents' sins...He was born blind so the power of God could be seen in him" (John 9:3 NLT).

The strangeness of Jesus' words echoes off the stone walls of the buildings that surround the scene. He explains that this man's eyes—which have never seen his mother's smile, never beheld the dazzling white marble of Herod's Temple reflecting the rays of the sun, never watched waves of wind wafting through the golden grain of a wheat field, never gazed on the face of a blushing young girl in love—have been dark all these years so the power of God can be seen in them today!

We watch—our attention is riveted on the man who has lived in darkness and the man who has called himself the light of the world. Jesus spits in the dust. No one speaks as he forms a mud pack in his carpenter's hands and patiently, tenderly spreads the mud over the blind man's eyes.

Jesus speaks. "Go wash yourself in the pool of Siloam" (John 9:7). What happens next defies natural explanation; it exceeds even the comprehension of twenty-first-century medical science. When the man obeys Jesus and washes the mud from his eyes, he can see![1]

The power of God was clearly demonstrated that day. But we see more than the miracle of bringing sight to the blind. We see the power of Jesus' compassion.

The expression used most often in Scripture to describe Jesus was that he was "moved with compassion." When he saw the blind, the lepers, the sick, and the hungry he was "moved with compassion" (see Matthew 9:36; 14:14; 15:32; 20:34; Mark 1:41; 6:34; 8:2). That day Jesus' heart of compassion was powerfully demonstrated because he saw the totality of the man's need. He saw him as a man in need physically (*he was blind*), in need economically (*he was begging*), in need emotionally (*beggars were looked down upon and at best pitied*), and in need spiritually (*he was a sinner*).

The disciples viewed this man through a spiritual inspecting lens—he was a sinner. Many today still wear those spiritual lenses. It's as if their "inspecting God" sees our sin first and foremost. But the accepting Jesus chooses to meet people at the point of their need of the moment, whether it is a spiritual or human need.

Jesus didn't say to the blind man, "If you don't believe in me as your Savior, then I'm not going to heal you." Later Jesus did in fact find the man and addressed his spiritual life, but he did so after he had healed him. Jesus didn't say to the lame man, "I'll make you a deal—I'll restore your legs to wholeness if you have a relationship with me." The power of Jesus' love and acceptance moved him to compassion for the human and spiritual needs of these people, and he set out to meet them both. This isn't to say God chooses to heal every affliction that we have; he obviously doesn't. But even in those situations, he is there to minister the power of his compassionate love and acceptance.

I (Sean) remember when I first began seminary. My plan was to coach basketball and teach Bible. I played four years of college basketball at Biola University and saw it as an amazing way to positively influence the lives of students.

Before we had kids my wife was teaching math at a local public high school. The head position for boys' basketball opened up at her school and I applied for it. I had worked out with the team the summer before and knew many of the players since my wife had been their teacher. I really wanted this coaching position! Even though I was young, I was confident I could motivate this team to success.

The school officials decided to give the position to a teacher who was on campus. Even though I understood their reasoning, I was disappointed not to have this position.

---

Jesus has given you his Word, in part, so you can have frequent fresh encounters with him to experience just how much he cares for you during your need of the moment.

---

What could be better than coaching at the school where my wife taught? In my disappointment someone directed me to Romans 8. I knew verse 28 by memory—"God causes everything to work together for the good of those who love God" (Romans 8:28). I knew in my head that I needed to trust in God's control. I knew I served a Sovereign God who had everything under control. But he wanted me to know more.

As I meditated on the passage it was as if God was saying to me "Sean, you are my child and I deeply care about what you're going through right now. I know you would love to have this coaching job. But trust me—I cause all things to work together for your good and my glory. And I do that because I know your future and have your best interest at heart."

I needed to see not only a Sovereign God at that moment, but also experience a caring God. Now that I look back on it I can see so many reasons why it would not have been good for me to get the coaching job. And I am struck anew with God's caring involvement in the details of my life.

Jesus has given you his Word, in part, so you can have frequent fresh encounters with him to experience just how much he cares for you during your need of the moment. Peter encourages you to "give all your worries and cares to God, for he cares about you" (1 Peter 5:7). Many Christians today wonder if Jesus' compassion can be experienced as those did who encountered him while he was on earth. You may think, *Well, he did make himself real and relevant to those he encountered, but how can his compassion be real and relevant to me through reading his Word?*

One of the keys to experiencing Jesus in Scripture is by asking the questions: "How does this text reveal the caring, compassionate heart of Jesus?" and "What is Jesus wanting me to experience from him right now?" With those two questions in mind, let us explore a few passages of Scripture.

## MARY'S ENCOUNTER WITH JESUS

Friendship was important to them, and Mary, Martha, and Lazarus (brother and sisters) had a dear friend in the person of Jesus. He had visited their home in Bethany numerous times, eating together and staying the night. Jesus knew he was welcome there anytime—they were close friends. You see, friendships were important to Jesus.

While Jesus was away, about a one-day journey from Bethany, Lazarus got deathly sick. The sisters sent word to Jesus telling him, "'Lord, the one you love is very sick'" (John 11:3 NLT).

But Jesus stayed where he was for another two days before heading to Bethany. By that time Lazarus had died. Yet the Master knew what he was going to do. "Our friend Lazarus has fallen asleep," Jesus said to his disciples, "but now I will go and wake him up" (verse 11). His purpose was clear; he was going to wake up the dead.

When Jesus arrived just outside Bethany, Martha came to meet him.

Mary stayed back at the house. By that time their brother had been dead four days. The first thing Martha said to Jesus when she saw him was, "Lord, if only you had been here, my brother would not have died" (John 11:21). She was obviously disappointed with Jesus.

She went back to Mary and told her Jesus wanted to see her too. When Mary went to him she fell at his feet weeping and said precisely what Martha had said, "Lord, if only you had been here, my brother would not have died" (verse 32).

The sisters clearly believed Jesus was the Messiah and the great healer. But now, from their perspective, it was too late. And Mary's tears may have, in part, reflected her disappointment that Jesus didn't come sooner. She knew she had lost her dear brother and Jesus couldn't do a thing about it now.

As his dear friend was shedding tears of sadness the Master did something extraordinary. Jesus wept. It is the shortest verse in the Bible. A simple but profound historical reality—Jesus wept. But why? Why would he be weeping? He knew that in a few minutes he was going to turn sorrow into joy by raising Lazarus from the dead. So what was he crying for—who was he crying for?

Jesus was weeping for and with his dear friend Mary. He loved her and it hurt him that she hurt. His heart was broken for her, and his tears of sorrow were meant to comfort her. Yes, he knew that just a few moments later she would be overwhelmed by joy by the sight of her resurrected brother. But for this moment in time the power of the compassionate Jesus was needed. And the great comforter met Mary at the point of her need of the moment. (See 2 Corinthians 1:24.)

Do you see how this short verse reveals the caring, comforting heart of God? Take a moment and reflect. Consider what he wants you to experience from him. Does he want you to feel his comforting arms? Do you know God at times weeps for you too? Or, does Jesus only weep for people named Mary? Could it be that when you encounter grief and sadness in your life, he is right there weeping with you? Is it true that he is "the same yesterday, today, and forever" (Hebrews 13:8)?

Let's explore a few more Scripture passages. Just before Jesus ascended into heaven he told his disciples, "Be sure of this: I am with you always, even to the end of the age" (Matthew 28:20). "When you believed in Christ," Paul said, "he identified you as his own by giving you the Holy Spirit, whom he [Jesus] promised long ago" (Ephesians 1:13). "His Holy Spirit speaks to us deep in our hearts and tells us that we are God's children" (Romans 8:16 NLT). Isn't this a part of the Holy Spirit's role as the "comforter"? To be there for you when you need him most?

And through the person of the Holy Spirit, isn't Jesus with you now? Does he not care what is going on in your life today? If that is true, and it surely is, then he weeps with you when you are grieving and in pain. At times you may be tempted to wonder where Jesus is, when you lose a loved one, struggle financially, experience a relational breakup, or suffer the pain of life's trials. Reality is, he is right there with you weeping with you, wanting to meet you at the point of your need of the moment. Can you reach out by faith and experience the comforting Jesus?

At times we all are tempted to say, like Mary and Martha, "Lord, if you had only been here sooner, then I wouldn't have had to go through this." He knows he is going to solve your problem soon. He is going to "put down all enemies of every kind" (1 Corinthians 15:24 NLT) and address all your problems so there "will be no more death or sorrow or crying or pain" (Revelation 21:4). But for the now, until that wonderful day comes, Jesus wants you to experience him as your caring, comforting friend for your need of the moment.

## PETER'S ENCOUNTER WITH JESUS

If ever there was an outspoken extrovert for Jesus, it was Peter. Without hesitation he left his career as a fisherman and followed Jesus (Matthew 4). When Jesus asked, "Who do you say that I am?" it was Peter who spoke up and declared Jesus as Christ—the Messiah (Matthew 16). It was also Peter who argued with Jesus when the Master began to tell of his pending trial and crucifixion (Mark 8).

Peter was among Jesus' inner circle. He would confide in Peter, along with James and John. He took them up to a mountain, known as the Mount of Transfiguration, and there Moses and Elijah appeared to them. Outspoken Peter was ready to pitch a sacred tent for Jesus, Moses, and Elijah (Matthew 17). He was always ready to go the second mile and do more than the others to show he was a Jesus-follower.

Peter was the one who climbed out of the boat to meet Jesus who was walking on the water (Matthew 14). He was the one who blurted out that he was unworthy for Jesus to wash his feet. And then when Jesus explained what it meant, Peter wanted Jesus to give him a bath! (John 13). Peter had his good traits, but he was impulsive, impatient, and overconfident. And in some ways perhaps that is what made him more vulnerable to temptation.

All the disciples abandoned Jesus at the time of his crucifixion, but not Peter—at least not at first. It was overconfident Peter who said, "I'm ready to die for you" (John 13:37) and took up his sword to prove he could defend Jesus (John 18). But when the pressure was on, in the moment of fear and temptation, rather than being known as a Christ-follower, Peter denied he knew Jesus (Mark 14).

Yet that was not the final story of Peter. He had failed more than once, and perhaps at the moment of his denial he felt like a total failure. But Jesus had not completed the portrait of the one he loved. When the angel announced to the women at the empty tomb that Jesus was risen, he told them to explain to the "disciples and Peter" that the risen Christ would appear to them (Mark 16). Jesus no doubt had the angel single out Peter by name to let him know he still loved and accepted him.

---

> No wonder Peter came through his trials and tests and eventually came out on top. Jesus, the Son of God, the Sovereign Lord of the universe and the Master miracle-worker, was praying specifically for him.

---

Peter would go on to be the demonstrative preacher on the day of Pentecost where some 3000 would come to believe in the Christ (Acts 2). He would go on to give healing to the crippled beggar, preach in the temple, be rescued from prison by an angel, and write two God-inspired letters to the church. In fact, it is in Peter's first letter that he provides incredible insights on how to overcome trials and temptation. Here is the man who denied his Messiah being inspired by God to proclaim truth about trials and temptations. "These trials," he said, "are only to test your faith, to show that it is strong and pure" (1 Peter 1:7 NLT).

Peter became a picture of endurance and strength. He eventually died a martyr's death, proud to give his life for the Master.

So what transformed an impetuous, overconfident, yet failing man into such a model of strength and courage for Christ? The key is in Peter's encounter with Jesus prior to his denial.

Just before Jesus tells Peter he will deny him he says, "Simon, Simon, Satan has asked to sift each of you like wheat. But I have pleaded in prayer for you, Simon, that your faith should not fail. So when you have repented and turned to me again, strengthen your brothers" (Luke 22:31-32). Wow! No wonder Peter came through his trials and tests and eventually came out on top. Jesus, the Son of God, the Sovereign Lord of the universe and the Master miracle-worker, was praying specifically for him. How could the Father not answer the prayers of his Son? Peter was on Jesus' prayer list. If God was for Peter, who could stand against him?

Take a moment to reflect. Does Jesus want you to succeed spiritually? Does he want you to overcome trials and temptations? Could he be praying for you too? Or...does he pray only for people named Peter? Could it be that when you are about to encounter trials, tests, and temptation Jesus is saying, "I am pleading in prayer for my child right now"? The apostle John says, "There is someone to plead for you before the Father. He is Jesus Christ, the one who pleases God completely" (1 John 2:1 NLT). And the Holy Spirit even prays so intensely that his groanings "cannot be expressed in words" (Romans 8:26).

What do these texts reveal about the caring, compassionate heart of Jesus? Do they not tell you that he believes in you? He is not about to give up on you, ever! He is praying that your faith will not fall short. Notice the confidence in Jesus' prayer for Peter: "So when you have repented and turned to me again." Jesus was sure that he was going to turn it around. It wasn't that he would never fail again. But in 50 days after Christ's death he would be empowered by the Holy Spirit. And through Christ he would be victorious to the end.

Jesus is that confident in his prayers for you too. The power of his Spirit is there to carry you through no matter what you are experiencing. And you will come out on the other end bringing glory to God, just as Peter did.

David Ferguson gives a challenge to us in his *Relational Foundations Workbook* on how we can respond like Peter did to Jesus' prayer.

> Peter's transformation from one who fearfully denied Christ to one who courageously witnessed at Pentecost gives evidence of his encounters with the real Jesus. We witness Peter's brokenness and tears of contrition when he looked into the eyes of Jesus immediately following the denial (Luke 22:61). We see how Christ took special notice of Peter after the Resurrection (Mark 16:7), and how he restored and commissioned him at the Sea of Tiberias (John 21:15-22). These encounters with the living Jesus helped prepare Peter to receive the divine empowerment of the Spirit that enabled him to boldly witness to the resurrected Christ on the day of Pentecost.
>
> Pause now and ask the Lord to bring additional boldness to your own life. Pray that he would reveal his special care for you, perhaps even in the midst of your own denial or abandonment of him. Ask him to show you how he takes special notice of you. Pray that his Spirit would bring any needed restoration to your life and ministry, empowering you with the same transforming power that Peter received.[2]

## HOW DOES JESUS WANT US TO SEE HIM?

The four Gospels reveal a compassionate Jesus who consistently met people at the point of their need. He wasn't big on talking about the future or dwelling on the past. He was the compassionate need-meeting Christ of the moment—addressing people and their needs at the time they had them. That is not to say that lessons of the past and hope for the future aren't important. But our God is the ever-present God. Jesus was even called "Immanuel," which means "God with us."

He is never too late, even though his timing doesn't always seem right to some. He never fails to fulfill a promise, even though some will need to be resurrected to claim them. He is a faithful and true friend who cares about children, hungry and hurting people, the sick and the dying. He came to give his life so that they, and all of us, could live—and live eternally.

But above all that, Jesus wants us to see him as our Lord and Savior who is with us now. Through the person and power of the Holy Spirit, Jesus is with us to pray for us, to weep with us, to bear our burdens, lift our load, strengthen us, and empower us to be his witness to a needy and lost world.

Through the miraculous power of God's Spirit, Jesus wants us to experience him on a daily basis. He wants his mind to be our mind. He wants his life to become our life. Jesus prayed to his Father for both his disciples and for us. He prayed, "They are not part of this world any more than I am. Make them pure and holy by teaching them your words of truth...My prayer for all of them is that they will be one, just as you and I are one, Father—that just as you are in me and I am in you, so they will be in us, and the world will believe you sent me" (John 17:16-17,21 NLT). Embrace the accepting and compassionate Jesus who is there to meet your need of the moment. He wants you to experience him.

A fitting close to this chapter is to add to Jesus' prayer the powerful prayer Paul gave for the followers of Christ at Ephesus. Read it carefully. Allow these God-breathed words to sink deep. Experience the real Jesus of Scripture.

> When I think of the wisdom and scope of God's plan, I fall to my knees and pray to the Father, the Creator of everything in heaven and on earth. I pray that from his glorious, unlimited resources he will give you mighty inner strength through his Holy Spirit. And I pray that Christ will be more and more at home in your hearts as you trust in him. May your roots go down deep into the soil of God's marvelous love. And may you have the power to understand, as all

God's people should, how wide, how long, how high, and how deep his love really is. May you experience the love of Christ, though it is so great you will never fully understand it. Then you will be filled with the fullness of life and power that comes from God.

Now glory be to God! By his mighty power at work within us, he is able to accomplish infinitely more than we would ever dare to ask or hope. May he be given glory in the church and in Christ Jesus forever and ever through endless ages. Amen (Ephesians 3:14-21 NLT).

# Chapter 5

# Experiencing Scripture with Others

Half of the shingles were blown off the barn. Some of the windows were broken. The siding on one side was almost gone, and what little paint remained on the trim was faded and peeling. The door was sagging, indicating the entire foundation was of questionable stability. Weeds of every kind overgrew the ground, which was caked with layers of dead leaves and windblown trash accumulated over the years.

I (Sean) stood there looking at the old place as my dad (Josh) swept his arm toward it and told my grown sisters and me that this was the 120-acre dairy farm he had called home when he was growing up just outside Union City, Michigan. I looked at the dilapidated barn, the precariously leaning corncrib, and the overgrown fields and tried to imagine what the place must have looked like in the early 1940s.

Dad could remember when his older sister would come home to visit and how he'd help make homemade ice cream on the back porch of the house. He said his mother made the best root beer in all of Michigan, and he had guzzled all the root-beer floats his parents would let him drink. Josh clearly saw more in this acreage than my sisters and I did. We saw a place in ruins; through the lens of memory he saw it as it once was.

As we walked toward the corncrib, Josh's entire demeanor changed. Pleasant thoughts of homemade ice cream and root beer quickly faded. The reality was, happy childhood memories for my father were few and far between. We were just a few feet from the old, leaning shed when he abruptly stopped. As he stared at the weather-beaten structure, memories touched a deep emotional wound made over 50 years ago.[1]

It was a Saturday morning. I (Josh) was 11 years old. I dressed before dawn and hurriedly got my morning chores done before the workmen arrived.

A team of men had been working for days to jack up a small house on my parents' farm, preparing it to be moved to a new location. My grown brother, Wilmont, was having it moved over the objections of my father. Wilmont had been engaged in a bitter feud with my dad, which had escalated into an all-out war for half of the family farm. Having successfully sued my father, Wilmont had arrived that morning with a sheriff, a deputy, and a court order authorizing him to move the house.

I, however, was trying hard to stay out of the conflict. I hated to see my dad and brother fight, but that was between them. Today I just wanted to savor the excitement of watching an entire house being towed down the road, a spectacle more entertaining to an 11-year-old mind than a traveling circus.

---

I ran from the shameful scene and into our nearby barn.
Slamming the door behind me, I scrambled into the
corn bin and buried myself up to my neck in corn.

---

Then, just as the tractors were being attached to the house, my father, drunk as usual, began yelling at Wilmont. The sheriff moved quickly toward the staggering man to prevent an ugly scene.

But it was too late for that. My brother, expecting something like this, had arranged for numerous families from our small farming community to be on hand to provide moral support for him. Many of them began chanting obscenities at my father as the sheriff restrained him.

I watched in horror, my excitement turning to embarrassment. Frightened by the escalating conflict and humiliated to see our family's feud played out in full view of my friends and neighbors, I ran from the shameful scene and into our nearby barn. Slamming the door behind me, I scrambled into the corn bin and buried myself up to my neck in corn.

As I lay in the dark, quiet and alone, my shame slowly turned to anger. I was angry that my father's drinking brought such division to my home. I was angry that he was rarely sober. And I was angry that he had caused such pain to my mother's life. But more than anything, I felt alone.

I lay there in the corn for what must have been hours. No one came looking for me. No one even seemed to notice I was gone. I felt forgotten and abandoned.[2]

Now, over five decades later, my dad seemed paralyzed by the memories of that terrible day. Tears began to trickle down his face. My sisters and I knew his story and immediately sensed what was going on with our father. We moved close to him and all three of us wrapped our arms around him. Dad wept openly, and we wept with him.

## HOW GOD MEETS RELATIONAL NEEDS

What was taking place that day between a hurting father and his three grown children? I (Sean) felt helpless to do anything about Josh's painful memories. And none of us had formal training in how to process a person through a traumatic experience in their past. This might seem to be a matter best left to God. For Scripture says that God "himself gives life and breath to everything, and he satisfies every need" (Acts 17:25). So it's clear that he does meet all our needs.

On the surface it appears we can be of no help to a hurting man who is reliving a painful memory. Perhaps this truly is a problem for God to handle on his own. He surely needs no assistance from us. Perhaps our job is to point Josh to the Great Physician who can heal all pain—past and present. Because honestly, isn't Jesus all we really need in life anyway? Some point to the apostle Paul's declaration that all his sufficiency was in Christ as proof that we only need Jesus: "I can do all this through him who gives me strength" (Philippians 4:13 NIV). So is that it? When people are hurting and in need do we simply point them to God?

Some people might also say that the Philippians passage implies we are spiritually weak if we need the support and aid of others, because God should be all-sufficient for us. But a full reading of the text proves otherwise. Notice what Paul says immediately after verse 13. "Yet it was good of you to share in my troubles…you sent me aid more than once when I was in need" (Philippians 4:14,16 NIV). Paul's message was, "I do everything through Christ, and he is pleased to involve you in that process." God is clearly the source of meeting our needs, yet he is pleased to involve others in his need-meeting ministry as channels of his strength and love.

In his book *The Never Alone Church*, David Ferguson points out, "It is clear from Christ's teachings and life that we need one another. In his unsearchable wisdom, God opted to meet our relational needs through a love relationship with both himself *and* other human beings. By divine order, we are created with a capacity to love and be loved by God and others. If either of these dimensions is missing, we are not ful-filling the Great Commandment."[3]

When my sisters and I were embracing Dad and weeping with him, he was getting more comfort than just what we were giving. God was supernaturally giving comfort through us to him as well. "He [God] comforts us in our troubles," Paul says, "so that we can comfort others. When they are troubled, we will be able to give them the same comfort God has given us" (2 Corinthians 1:4).

Everyone at some point suffers physical, emotional, or spiritual dif-ficulties in life. And we can be there to experience Romans 12:15 with them to "mourn with those who mourn" (NIV). We become God's chan-nel of comfort and healing to those who are hurting. At that point the person not only senses our comforting words and touch, but also that of God himself. It is not that he can't directly comfort those who are hurt-ing—he does. It is that he additionally is pleased to administer some of his comfort through us to others. As Paul said, "We are Christ's ambas-sadors, and God is using us to speak to you" (2 Corinthians 5:20 NLT).

## EXPERIENCING THE "ONE ANOTHERS" OF SCRIPTURE

When we follow the admonition of Romans 12:15b—"mourn

with those who mourn"—we are actually experiencing the scriptural truth that we are to comfort one another. There are many such biblical truths that appear as "one another" passages of Scripture. At least 35 times in the New Testament, we see a recurring word pattern—an action verb followed by the words "one another." When we literally experience those Bible passages with others we are living and loving as Christ loves us. Paul says, "as the Spirit of the Lord works within us, we become more and more like him reflecting his glory even more" (2 Corinthians 3:18 NLT).

We know, for example, the nature of Jesus' love was gentle, humble, and forgiving. Scripture admonishes us to live out those characteristics of Christ by being gentle to one another (Ephesians 4:2), being humble toward one another (1 Peter 5:5), and forgiving one another (Colossians 3:13). By identifying these "one another" passages, we get a much clearer picture of what words of Scripture God would be pleased for us to experience with family, friends, and the world around us. Consider the following list of Scriptures that can be experienced with others.

Experience the "One Anothers" of Scripture

1. Love one another (John 13:34).
2. Accept one another (Romans 15:7).
3. Forgive one another (Ephesians 4:32; Colossians 3:13).
4. Be gentle to one another (Ephesians 4:2).
5. Be clothed in humility toward one another (1 Peter 5:5).
6. Weep with one another (Romans 12:15).
7. Live in harmony with one another (Romans 12:16).
8. Don't judge one another (Romans 14:13).
9. Be patient with one another (Ephesians 4:2).
10. Admonish one another (Colossians 3:16).
11. Greet one another (Romans 16:16).
12. Wait for one another (1 Corinthians 11:33).
13. Care for one another (1 Corinthians 12:25).
14. Serve one another (Galatians 5:13).

15. Be kind to one another (Ephesians 4:32).

16. Be devoted to one another (Romans 12:10).

17. Be compassionate toward one another (Ephesians 4:32).

18. Encourage one another (1 Thessalonians 5:11).

19. Submit to one another (Ephesians 5:21).

20. Make allowances for one another (Colossians 3:13).

21. Stimulate love in one another (Hebrews 10:24).

22. Offer hospitality to one another (1 Peter 4:9).

23. Use your gifts to serve one another (1 Peter 4:10).

24. Rejoice with one another (Romans 12:15;
    1 Corinthians 12:26).

25. Don't slander one another (James 4:11).

26. Don't grumble against one another (James 5:9).

27. Confess your sins to one another (James 5:16).

28. Pray for one another (James 5:16).

29. Fellowship with one another (1 John 1:7).

30. Don't be puffed up against one another (1 Corinthians 4:6).

31. Carry one another's burdens (Galatians 6:2).

32. Honor one another (Romans 12:10).

33. Depend on one another (Romans 12:5 AMP)

34. Prefer one another (Romans 12:10).

35. Comfort one another (2 Corinthians 1:4).

## MY STRUGGLE TO EXPERIENCE GALATIANS 6:2

As we discussed in chapters 3 and 4, in order to experience the real Jesus of Scripture we must gain an accurate biblical view of Christ. We must lay aside the distorted lenses often created by past or present human relationships and allow the Holy Spirit through Scripture to present us a clear picture of who God is and how he views us. The same is true in experiencing Bible verses with others. We must unpackage the textual and relational meanings of these "one another" passages to effectively live them out.

Take, for example, Galatians 6:2, where we are to carry one another's burdens. Because of some dysfunctional relationships in my (Josh's) early years, I had a misconception about this verse.

I grew up in the home of an alcoholic, and I developed a pattern of behavior that made me what psychologists call a "rescuer." Each time I saw my father try to hurt my mom, I would step in and try to prevent her from being hurt. This became a lifelong psychological and emotional pattern for me. I always tried to rescue hurting, struggling people.

---

We all face situations that bear down heavily on us,
and God is pleased that others experience Galatians 6:2 with
us by coming alongside to support us in our difficulty.

---

When I became a Christian I continued this unhealthy behavioral pattern, though I didn't realize it was unhealthy. Each time I saw someone hurting, my compulsion kicked in. But I didn't know it was a compulsion; I thought it was compassion. I thought I was exhibiting Godlike love. When I read the passage "bear one another's burdens, and thereby fulfill the law of Christ" (Galatians 6:2 NASB), I felt emotionally responsible to solve the person's problem by removing whatever burden they had. I thought I was fulfilling the "law of Christ" and acting as he would. In reality, I was doing myself harm and in most cases doing the person a disservice, all because I was seeing God's love through my dysfunctional "rescuing" lenses.

It took the help of others for me to see this passage clearly. I learned that Scripture doesn't teach that bearing another person's burden means taking responsibility for that person's problem or hurt. Rather, it means coming alongside and gently helping a person lift the weight. Bearing the burdens of others doesn't mean *taking responsibility for their problem*; it means *being responsible to them*—to comfort, encourage, and support them in their pain or difficulties.

Yes, Galatians 6:2 tells us that we are to "bear one another's burdens."

The key to my turnaround was the passage I discovered just three more verses down the page. Galatians 6:5 declares, "Each one will bear his own load" (NASB).

Now, this may sound confusing at first, but it comes together when you consider that there is an important difference between a "burden" and a "load." The Greek word for burden is *baros,* which denotes a heavy weight. Jesus used this word when describing the workers toiling in the vineyard who have "borne the burden (*baros*) and the scorching heat of the day" (Matthew 20:12 NASB). This was a heavy burden to bear.

We all face situations that bear down heavily on us, and God is pleased that others experience Galatians 6:2 with us by coming alongside to support us in our difficulty. Consider the image of a man carrying a heavy beam across his shoulders. Now watch as two friends come alongside him. They put their shoulders on either side of the beam and help lift his load. That is the picture here. When we are burdened down with an injury, an illness, the loss of a job, or loss of a loved one, we need support; we need others to help us lift our heavy load.

In verse 5 Paul uses a different word for burden or weight. He says, "Each one shall bear his own load" (Galatians 6:5 NASB). This is the Greek word *phortion,* which refers to something with little weight that is carried, like a supply pack a first-century soldier would carry into the field. A more natural term is given in the New Living Translation: "We are each responsible for our own conduct" (Galatians 6:5). In other words, this load is your assignment, and bearing it is your responsibility alone. It's the idea Paul was conveying when he said, "Each of us will give a personal account to God" (Romans 14:12).

We all have personal responsibilities, and when we fail in our responsibilities—by using poor judgment or making wrong choices or harboring bad attitudes—we must face up to the consequences. To step in and remove the natural and corrective consequences of people's irresponsible behavior may rob them of valuable lessons—lessons which may be critical for their continued growth and maturity.

I can't possibly express how valuable this revelation from God's Word has been to me. When I realized that experiencing Galatians 6:2 with others didn't mean I was responsible *for* other people, then I was set free to be responsible *to* others—and particularly to those who were hurting. I then began looking for opportunities to allow God's compassionate encouragement and support to flow through me to others. Then I knew that in doing this I was experiencing Galatians 6:2 with others as God designed.[4]

## WHEN SOMEONE EXPERIENCED HEBREWS 10:24 WITH ME

Have you ever been discouraged and just feeling down? We all face disappointments in life and can even lose hope for a period of time. Not long ago I (Sean) became discouraged and was in need of a lift.

After I got my ministry website up and running I began to blog and post articles on current topics of interest to youth and youth leaders. Many of them dealt with biblically informed ethical decisions facing today's young people. And some of those issues can be quite controversial.

I've always believed we should never compromise on the truth of God's Word. Yet in taking a stand we must always "speak the truth in love, growing in every way more and more like Christ" (Ephesians 4:15). And I had done my best to do that, especially realizing a lot of people who do not share my values would be reading my postings.

A friend of mine had gotten hold of one of my talks on video and decided to send it out to hundreds of youth pastors. The problem is that he selected about 60 seconds of what I had to say at length on a controversial subject. My friend meant well and was trying to help me, but my comments were clearly out of context. And consequently I got severely criticized.

Now I have been criticized in the past, but this was different. I was attacked for being ignorant, manipulative, hateful, un-Christian, a fearmonger—you name it. I knew I was none of those things and if people had seen my entire talk they would know that too. So I felt unjustly criticized.

At first I was dazed by the onslaught. It hurt—and honestly, tears welled up in my eyes as I told Stephanie about it. She, of course, was there to comfort me, and I should have just moved on. But I struggled with being misunderstood, and I became discouraged.

I decided to send out a message on Twitter that asked, "How do you get thicker skin so criticism falls off you like water off a duck's back?" A friend contacted me and said, "Sean, I don't think you want thick skin. Suffering is the badge of a true disciple." And then he directed me to what Peter had to say: "Be happy if you are insulted for being a Christian, for then the glorious Spirit of God will come upon you…it is no shame to suffer for being a Christian. Praise God for the privilege of being called by his wonderful name!…So if you are suffering according to God's will, keep on doing what is right, and trust yourself to the God who made you, for he will never fail you" (1 Peter 4:14,16,19).

What had my friend done? He lifted my spirits, he urged me toward a positive goal, he provided me with words of encouragement. And he experienced Hebrews 10:24 with me:

> Think of ways to encourage one another to outbursts of love and good deeds (NLT).

I, of course, was aware of 1 Peter 4. But the truth of that passage didn't become real to me until God granted his encouragement through a faithful friend willing to experience Hebrews 10:24 with me.

## OTHER SCRIPTURES TO EXPERIENCE WITH OTHERS

We all have the need for comfort, support, and encouragement. And when we experience Romans 12:15b, Galatians 6:2, and 1 Corinthians 12:25 with those around us the "Spirit of the Lord works within us" to meet people at the point of their need.

David Ferguson has identified over 50 relational needs in Scripture. We will simply mention 10 that he covers extensively in his book *The Never Alone Church*. The better we understand these relational "one another" needs the better we can understand how God wants to work through us to meet the needs of those around us. Following are definitions of these relational needs and the applicable Scripture passages we can experience with others.

### Experiencing the "one another" need for comfort.

Giving hope; easing a grief or pain; consoling and hurting with a person.

He [God] is the source of every mercy and the God who comforts us. He comforts us in all our troubles so that we can comfort others (2 Corinthians 1:3-4 NLT).

### Experiencing the "one another" need for support.

Coming alongside another to lift a load and help carry a problem.

Carry each other's burdens, and in this way you will fulfill the law of Christ (Galatians 6:2 NIV).

### Experiencing the "one another" need for attention (care).

Taking thought of another, conveying interest and concern, entering another's world.

All the members [of the church] care for each other equally (1 Corinthians 12:25 NLT).

### Experiencing the "one another" need for appreciation.

Praising another and communicating gratefulness through words and deeds.

I praise you for remembering me in everything (1 Corinthians 11:2 NIV).

### Experiencing the "one another" need for acceptance.

Acceptance without conditions by loving others for who they are.

Accept each other just as Christ has accepted you; then God will be given glory (Romans 15:7).

### Experiencing the "one another" need for security.

Eliminating danger and removing the fear of loss, want, and broken relationship.

Perfect love expels all fear (1 John 4:18).

### Experiencing the "one another" need for approval.

Expressing satisfaction with a person; demonstrating that he or she has pleased another.

If you serve Christ with this attitude, you will please God. And other people will approve of you, too (Romans 14:18 NLT).

### Experiencing the "one another" need for affection.

Communicates care and closeness by offering endearing words and appropriate physical touch.

Love each other with genuine affection (Romans 12:10).

### Experiencing the "one another" need for encouragement.

Inspiring with courage and urging another forward to a positive goal.

Encourage one another to outbursts of love and good deeds (Hebrews 10:24 NLT).

### Experiencing the "one another" need for respect.

Valuing a person highly and communicating to that person that he or she is of great worth.

Show respect for everyone (1 Peter 2:17 NLT).

## SIMPLE, BUT NOT NECESSARILY EASY

The apostle Paul challenges us to "be diligent [in]…accurately handling the word of truth" (2 Timothy 2:15 NASB). God's truth is profoundly simple but not necessarily easy to live and experience with others. David Ferguson reminds us of this point:

Experiencing God's Word with others in order to express Great Commandment love and meet relational needs is profoundly simple. God has filled his written Word with instructions and examples for our attitudes, words, and actions. But the daily practice of experiencing his Word and helping others do the same is not necessarily easy. It requires spiritual discipline—staying in tune with God, allowing the Holy Spirit to minister to us and through us, saying no to the flesh, and living out our identity in Christ. When we experience his Word, we are in effect taking on

Christ's loving character and acting out his nature. Being conformed to Christ's image is the daily disciplined process of loving God and living out his Word in our relationships. But Jesus reminds us that we have freely received God's grace and we are called to freely pass his love on to others.[5]

Take time this week to review the list of "one another" needs and Scripture passages and "give as freely as you have received" (Matthew 10:8). Look for opportunities to experience God's book with others. God has given you his Holy Spirit to both supply your needs and to work through you to help meet the needs of others. You are part of Christ's living body—the church—and he is saying to you and a needy world...

- There is *comfort* to ease your physical hurts, to provide a shoulder to cry on, and to produce inner healing.

- There is *attention* (care) that communicates that you are so important to God that he died to have a relationship with you, and his church is here to help address all your human and spiritual needs.

- There is *acceptance* that says you are loved for who you are, no matter what.

- There is *appreciation* that praises you for who you are and what you've done.

- There is *support* when you need a helping hand or a shoulder to help you carry a heavy load.

- There is *encouragement* when you are struggling with disappointments, failure, or difficulty.

- There is *affection* to help you know that through it all, you are truly loved.

- There is *approval* that says, "I am pleased with you."

- There is *security* in times of danger to remove your fear of the future.

- There is *respect* that honors you for what you think and values you for the contribution you bring.[6]

We close with Paul's challenge:

> Since God chose you to be the holy people whom he loves, you must clothe yourselves with tenderhearted mercy, kindness, humility, gentleness, and patience. You must make allowance for each other's faults and forgive the person who offends you. Remember, the Lord forgave you, so you must forgive others. And the most important piece of clothing you must wear is love. Love is what binds us all together in perfect harmony. And let the peace that comes from Christ rule in your hearts. For as members of one body you are all called to live in peace. And always be thankful.
>
> Let the words of Christ, in all their richness, live in your hearts and make you wise. Use his words to teach and counsel each other. Sing psalms and hymns and spiritual songs to God with thankful hearts. And whatever you do or say, let it be as a representative of the Lord Jesus, all the while giving thanks through him to God the Father (Colossians 3:12-17 NLT).

# Chapter 6

# The Key to Discovering the Truth

She wanted to prepare a big dinner for her special guest. There were so many details to attend to. Her sister, Mary, was supposed to be helping, but instead she was sitting at the feet of Jesus listening to what he had to say.

So Martha marched in and said to Jesus, "'Lord, doesn't it seem unfair to you that my sister just sits here while I do all the work? Tell her to come and help me.' But the Lord said to her, 'My dear Martha, you are worried and upset over all these details! There is only one thing worth being concerned about. Mary has discovered it, and it will not be taken away from her'" (Luke 10:40-42).

Life is full of details. We can't seem to live a day without dealing with them, and often worrying about them. "What am I going to wear today?" "What is on my plate at work today?" "Where are the kids, are they doing okay, what are they getting into?" "What do I need to buy, and is it in our budget—what budget?" "What's happening next week?" "When are things going to slow down?" "When am I going to get time for me, for us?"

Life these days moves at a rapid pace. We live in a more complex world than previous generations, aided and abetted by all our new technologies. And our complex lives can sometimes cause confusion, concern, and even anxiety over all the details. Life these days isn't simple, and it can be more than a little messy.

But Jesus brought focus to the messy details of life when he said,

"There is only one thing worth being concerned about" (verse 42). What was that one thing? Mary had discovered it. She seemed to be asking the right questions and seeking the right answers to life. More important, she was asking and seeking from the right person. But what was that one thing?

## CULTIVATING A HEART OF RELATIONAL DISCOVERY

Mary was in the room sitting at Jesus' feet. She was in a transparent, receiving posture. That "one thing" that was worth everything to her was the passionate pursuit of a deepened relationship with Jesus. It involved far more than exploring the doctrinal meaning to his teachings. It was even more than understanding how to apply his commandments to her life. She was captivated by the lifelong journey to know Jesus more deeply for who he really was, and she was willing to allow him to know her for who she was. Mary had found that one thing; it was a heart of relational discovery. She was in love with her God and sought to be part of his kingdom.

---

The marriage relationships that stay fresh and alive involve two people who continually seek to know each other. They are on an ever-deepening journey of relational discovery.

---

I (Sean) remember how my thought process and entire life changed after meeting this stunning girl named Stephanie. Yes, I was struck by her beauty, but it was more than that. She was smart and funny and had a great personality. She and I liked a lot of the same things, and I wanted to be with her all the time. When I was at basketball practice I thought about her. When I was in school I thought about her. When I was at home I thought about her. I couldn't get her out of my mind, because she had made a place deep in my heart.

It seemed that every waking moment this woman captivated my thoughts. There was more to it than I could really understand. There was a mystery to this consuming passion of mine. I knew her and yet

I didn't, so I wanted to know her more. And the more I knew her the more I wanted to know her. *Because I was deeply in love!*

After Stephanie and I married, the love affair deepened further. In fact, our togetherness created a home of our own for us. While marriage meant we could spend a lot of time together, I still had to be away at times. She didn't like me being away. She became a little jealous of my time when I was at work or at the seminary too long. At times I had to travel to a speaking engagement. Of course, I would e-mail her and call her. But it wasn't the same. She missed me and wanted me home. And I liked it that she did. I missed her too. We just couldn't get enough of each other.

I'm not a marriage expert, but from time to time my students do ask me things like "How can you know if you're really in love?" and "How do you make love last?" My parents have been married for over 40 years and they are still deeply in love too. So I have made some observations about marriages that last. This is what I've observed: The marriage relationships that stay fresh and alive involve two people who continually seek to know each other. They are on an ever-deepening journey of relational discovery.

I will spend a lifetime discovering this woman called Stephanie and never really know her fully. There is still a mystery about the deep essence and inner being of this woman that causes me to want to know her more. She still has the power to allure me, intrigue me, and captivate my heart because I never have and never will stop pursuing her. And the more I pursue her, the more I want to pursue her. That is the true nature of a love relationship.

You have probably heard about the couple who had gone to a marriage counselor because the wife didn't feel like her husband loved her. When asked why, the wife said, "He never tells me he loves me anymore." The counselor turned to the man and asked, "Is that true?" The husband replied, "I told her I loved her the day we got married and I figured one tellin' is enough."

That is not the true nature of a love relationship. It is not a destination. Love doesn't happen on a wedding day that is sealed by a marriage vow. Love is a decision to embark on a journey of devotion and discovery. It is a heart in pursuit of the one you love for a lifetime and beyond. Love has an insatiable appetite to know more and more of the person it is pursuing. True love loves and keeps on loving. This is the kind of love God wants of us toward him. He wants us to love him with a heart of relational discovery—to discover him and keep on discovering him.

When Jesus' disciples asked him to teach them about prayer, he didn't just give them a set of words to recite, as if to say, "Pray these words once and you have arrived." Rather, he taught his disciples to ask and "keep on asking, and you will receive what you ask for. Keep on seeking, and you will find. Keep on knocking, and the door will be opened to you" (Luke 11:9). God wants to cultivate within us a searching heart, a spirit of discovery, an ever-hungry soul that longs for him more and more. And when we find him, he does satisfy us while at the same time deepening our hunger to know him more. That is what Mary had found—and Jesus said, "It won't be taken away from her."

The psalmist David followed this same love pursuit for God. He knew who his God was, but he remained in constant search of him:

> O God, you are my God; I earnestly search for you. My soul thirsts for you; my whole body longs for you in this parched and weary land where there is no water. I have seen you in your sanctuary and gazed upon your power and glory. Your unfailing love is better than life itself; how I praise you! (Psalm 63:1-3).

> As the deer pants for streams of water, so I long for you, O God. I thirst for God, the living God (Psalm 42:1-2 NLT).

It is not that Martha was wrong in fixing a meal for her Master or even in getting a little concerned over the details. We have to deal with the details of life. But the primary thing in life, the most important thing, is to be in pursuit of God as the primary love of our lives. If our pursuit is for selfish pleasure or we give our dedication to the things of this world, God actually gets jealous. The apostle James wrote, "If your aim is to enjoy this world, you can't be a friend of God. What do you think the Scriptures mean when they say that the Holy Spirit, who God has placed within us, jealously longs for us to be faithful?" (James 4:4-5 NLT). How do you respond to the thought that God jealously loves you? He wants you to love him exclusively, just like you want someone to make you "number one" in his or her life.

God created us in his image, so we as humans don't respond well to someone being unfaithful to us either, do we? We want to know that we are "exclusive" in the heart and mind of the person that loves us. And when we sense the affection that we were promised is being directed somewhere else, we get jealous. The nature of loving relationships is about making the object of our love the number-one priority.

Stephanie wants me to think about her while I am away just like I want her to think about me. And if other things take my devotion away from her she will be hurt—as she should be. God too jealously longs for us to long for him. He wants our deep devotion, and as we give it to him he increases our longing to know him more. As we search to know him through his Word, he wants us to keep on searching. As we discover his transforming truth in the pages of Scripture, he wants us to keep on discovering. For as we cultivate a heart of discovery to know him and his ways, he will guide us into knowing and being and living in ever-deepening oneness with him.

The apostle Paul said, "We don't even know what we should pray for, nor how we should pray. But the Holy Spirit prays for us with groaning that cannot be expressed in words. And the Father who knows all hearts knows what the Spirit is saying" (Romans 8:26-27 NLT). Paul goes on in Corinthians to talk about the deep secret wisdom of God and that "God has revealed it to us by his Spirit. The Spirit searches all things, even the deep things of God" (1 Corinthians 1:10 NIV). We serve a God who has provided us with his Word and given us his Spirit to guide us into those words. He doesn't want us to worry about the things of this world. He wants us to cultivate an ever-increasing longing to know him deeply within the pages of Scripture. He wants us to love him and "make the Kingdom of God your primary concern" (Matthew 6:33).

The key to discovering truth then is in *cultivating a heart of relational discovery*. But such a discovery is enhanced by the questions we ask. In other words, a person with a heart for relationship also needs an inquiring mind that wants to know.

## SEEKING ANSWERS BY ASKING THE RIGHT QUESTIONS

Early in my (Josh's) ministry with Campus Crusade for Christ I was assigned to Argentina. Imagine my culture shock when I discovered that their favorite sport was not American football or basketball, but soccer. The first time I watched a soccer game, I was utterly confused. I had no idea what was going on. I was totally ignorant of the rules, the strategy, or even what was supposed to happen on the field. But after seeing several soccer matches and listening to explanations, I learned the rules and the subtleties of player moves and strategy. I began to anticipate plays, and even shouted advice to the players—and the referees. I learned what to look for, and that knowledge increased my appreciation and enjoyment of the game tremendously.

The same is true for discovering the deep things of God within the pages of Scripture. If we don't learn some of the ins and outs of what the book is about, we will not know what to look for. Then we may find the Bible confusing and uninteresting. But when we learn to see beneath the surface of the words of the Bible, the many facets of God's revelation will begin to unfold to us. It is crucial, therefore, that a seeking heart learn the right questions to ask. Then with the guidance of the Holy Spirit, we can begin to understand what God wants to reveal to us.

Learning to ask the right questions actually helps us see what is really there. To illustrate, the FBI uses training films to teach agents the art of observation. One of these films is three minutes long and shows a train robbery. Accompanying the film is a list of over 100 questions testing what agents observe on seeing the film for the first time. The list includes such questions as "Was the man left-handed?" "What was in his back pocket?" "Did the woman wear a watch?" and so on.

A seminary professor once showed this film in his class on Bible-study methods. The average score was 35 correct answers to the more than 100 questions. But one year an ex-FBI agent took the professor's course. He had never seen that particular training film, yet he answered every question correctly. What was the key? He knew what to look for by asking the right questions.

> The Bible is a mysterious book, and it requires a heart of discovery to peer into its depths to experience its richness. But the rewards are tremendously satisfying.

So not knowing the right questions hinders our discovery process. We also need to know *how* to look. If we don't know how to look into the Bible we can lose motivation and simply quit looking. We may read a passage, but we can fail to see the meaning of what we read. I know people who miss the meaning of great art because they don't know how to look at a painting. You've seen it happen in museums. One group of visitors will pass a painting and shake their heads and laugh or make a glib wisecrack about it. The next group will stop and gaze at the same painting in breathless awe, excitedly discussing with each other the meaning and impact of the piece.

Why such different responses? The second group knows how to see a painting. They understand such things as movement, form, gesture, harmony, and composition—all the elements that make a painting communicate. That is why you sometimes hear people say that we don't judge paintings; paintings judge us. The same can be said of those who claim they can't get anything out of the Bible.

Another hindrance in the discovery process is simply a failure to look. Once some people realize truth is not just going to pop off the page, they close the book and abandon the effort. They fail to look, therefore they do not see. Like we stated earlier, the Bible is a mysterious book, and it requires a heart of discovery to peer into its depths to experience its richness. But the rewards are tremendously satisfying because by knowing God and his ways we find meaning, purpose, and fulfillment in this life, not to mention eternal life.

## SIX BASIC QUESTIONS

We discover how to look and what to look for in Scripture by learning to ask the right questions. These are six basic questions to ask that will help us uncover the truths of many things. Crime investigators use these questions. Prosecutors and defense lawyers use these questions. Scientists use these questions. Journalists ask these questions. They are:

Who?

What?

When?

Where?

Why?

How?

Never mind that this seems elementary. It is these questions that force us to penetrate the surface and dig out the doctrinal, behavioral, and relational truth of a passage. These are the questions that helped us to see what was really there in previous chapters about the Pharisees asking Jesus questions, Jesus' answers, the Samaritan woman at the well, Jesus healing the blind man, Jesus' encounter with Mary, the "one anothers" of Scripture, and so on. These questions actually helped us bring to the surface the information and truth that was not immediately obvious. They are like spades used in digging for buried treasure. They probe down into a passage and unearth the hidden thoughts and meaning so we can experience God more deeply or experience the truths of God's Word in the lives of others.

For example, let's take these six questions and apply them to Jesus' meeting the woman at the well, which we discussed in chapter 3. By answering these questions we will see how they helped us uncover the rich truths we experienced from John 4.

**"Who"** uncovers the personalities involved. Who is Jesus in the passage of John 4:1-42? We found he is the accepting Jesus. Who was the woman? We found she was a Samaritan who Jews didn't associate with, an adulterer who had many husbands, and a lonely woman who needed unconditional acceptance.

**"Where"** helps us with direction. Where did the event described happen? Where are the characters involved going? In John 4 we uncover that Jesus is going to Galilee, but he goes by the way of Samaria. The meeting between Jesus and the woman takes place in Samaria at a well, which is significant. In this case, it is where Jesus is revealing his accepting, caring heart.

**"When"** questions bring the dimension of time into play. We realize Jesus is going through Samaria at a time when Jews just didn't travel there, and for "good reason." The tensions between Jews and Samaritans were clear—they despised each other. When did the woman come to the well? It was at noontime, which we learn was a time when others were not there drawing water. This is significant, and the "when" question helps us discover that she didn't want people to see her. She obviously was a lonely woman who was looked down on because of her adulterous lifestyle.

**"What"** uncovers much in a passage. What are the verses saying? What is happening? What did he do, what did she do? What are the motives here? What is Jesus doing offering this outcast living water? What makes Jesus want to be the Messiah to this woman? What must have gone through the woman's mind? What is Jesus wanting you to experience from him as a result of this story or truth? What do you see about Jesus' heart of acceptance that relates to you? What is your response to an accepting Jesus in your life?

**"How"** involves the process of the events, feelings, emotions, relationships, and so on. How has the event of a passage happened? Or, how could it happen? How will it happen? How did Jesus know this woman had five husbands? How did the woman respond to Jesus' offer to her? How did she respond to his knowing the details of her life? How would you feel if Jesus accepted you that way? How does this reveal his caring, compassionate heart? How do you receive his acceptance of you? How does this prompt you to better accept yourself? How do you accept others the way Jesus accepted the Samaritan woman? How does this passage help lead you into a deeper love of God and a deeper love of others?

**"Why"** questions help us dig deeper into the motives and reasons behind the text. Why did Jesus ask her for a drink? Why did he go there in the first place? Why is this woman coming in the middle of the afternoon to draw water? Why does Jesus care so much for the outcasts? Why would Jesus accept you without condition? Why would you accept others like Jesus accepts you?

Asking the right questions then becomes a major tool for you to unlock scriptural truths. Questions become your personal probes to discover, for example, doctrinal insights into who God is and what he is like. They can guide you into a deep understanding of what to believe. These questions will allow you to uncover the ways of God that are to be followed. And of course, these questions will allow you to understand the reason God gave you his Word—so you can enjoy a deepened relationship with him and those around you.

♒

In the next part we will walk you through this process to help you dig out the deeper truths of Scripture for yourself. There are of course helpful tools like Greek and Hebrew word studies, various translations written as study Bibles, Bible dictionaries, and a host of other helps. All these will add to your personal discovery of God's Word. And while we will focus much of our journey within the New Testament, we will not overlook the Old Testament. The Old Testament is rich in transforming truth. The Hebrew text is more than the story of the family line of Jesus—the children of Israel. It represents the story of all of us. In fact our own story is not complete and we don't get the full impact of God's message to us without both the Old and New Testaments.

In many respects, the Bible from the first verse of Genesis to the last verse in Revelation provides the sweeping story of the human race, its dilemma, and an offered solution. Often we don't see clearly where we fit within that story. With the right tools, motivation, and guidance from the Holy Spirit you can find your place within each text and experience the Bible for yourself.

In some respects, we will shift gears in this next part. We will be asking you to dig into various passages by asking the right questions and providing space for you to respond. We will still provide direction, offer insight we have discovered, and even insights that others have uncovered. But our hope is that this first part has provided a context so you can begin experiencing the Bible on your own. And in the next part we provide you an opportunity to do so. Let the journey continue.

# PART TWO

# How to Experience the Bible for Yourself

# Chapter 7

# Interpretation:
## Understanding the Intended Meaning

ary has just finished reading 2 Peter 1:3-4 to the group gathered for Bible study. He turns to Marci, who is sitting right next to you, and asks, "What do these verses mean?"

Marci, a professed Christian, pauses to reflect on the passage. "Well," she begins after a few moments of careful consideration, "What these verses mean to me is that God is there to help me live the Christian life." Gary nods and says, "That's good." He looks right at you. "What do these verses mean to you?"

Chances are you wouldn't even detect the subtle shift in meaning between Gary's first question and Marci's response. But look again. The importance of the words "means to me" and "mean to you" must not be minimized. They are indicative of a condition that exists among most Christians today. Many people are not looking to the biblical text in order to know *the* meaning of the truth; they are actually looking for *their* meaning of the truth.

The vast majority of our culture, including many professed Christians, says there is no objective moral truth. What such people are saying is that there is no moral truth that stands apart from the individual, who defines and determines what is right or wrong, true or false. For them, truth is subjectively or personally created. They believe an individual determines what is right or true for him or her. Therefore, the best we can do with the Bible is to use it as a guide to determine a personal "truth" that is arrived at via our own ideas and preferences.

Recently *Time* magazine did a cover story on a theological position long held by the early church, one that is rooted firmly in Scripture. The article was written by Jon Meacham, former editor for *Newsweek*, who is said to be "one of America's foremost thinkers on the role of religion in public life."[1]

---

In today's subjective-truth culture, theology is a matter of human opinions and preferences and therefore not really open to debate.

---

What theological topic was being addressed was not as significant as the cultural mind-set in which it was being discussed. Rather than looking to Scripture as the authority on theology, Meacham declared, "Like the Bible—a document that often contradicts itself and from which one can construct sharply different arguments—theology is the product of human hands and hearts."[2]

If in fact the Bible is a contradictory hodgepodge of ideas and teachings that cannot be considered to have authoritatively come from the mind and heart of God, we would definitely agree with Meacham that theology is the product of our own individual thinking. But if the Bible can be trusted (see chapter 12) as having come from an immutable God then he, not we, determines theology. Debate on theology is healthy when the parties agree that the Bible is the authoritative word on the subject. But in today's subjective-truth culture, theology is a matter of human opinions and preferences and therefore not really open to debate. And if anyone is so bold as to state that a truth is objectively and authoritatively true, they are considered at minimum out of date and at worst a bigot.

I (Sean) was speaking at a youth rally on the topic of sexuality. In the middle of my talk a girl interrupted and echoed the five words I so often hear from young people today: "Who are you to judge?" She was saying I had no right to make moral judgments because truth is subjective—that is, it was "my truth"—which makes all views equal. This girl, like most of us, has grown up in a culture of moral relativism, which prides itself on accepting many "truths." We have been told we need to be tolerant of all beliefs, without rendering judgment, without being critical, and to think that no one way is better than another and no theological viewpoint is more right than another. In fact, the moment anyone claims to know the truth as presented in God's Word, he or she is labeled irrelevant, bigoted, and judgmental.

While we reject the idea that truth is personal and subjective, it isn't totally incorrect—and that causes some people confusion. Because, in fact, some truth is a personal choice or preference. For example, which statement is true: "Chocolate is the best flavor of ice cream" or "Vanilla is the best flavor of ice cream"? Your answer would depend on your taste preference, and thus it would be neither right nor wrong, neither true nor untrue. Chocolate can be the best to you, and vanilla can be the best to me. There is no contradiction here because we are talking about our subjective preferences. This kind of truth is relative to the individual and can change.

But when it comes to the Bible, authored by God who is the absolute standard of moral truth, that's another issue. God's Word is a revelation of and from the one who defines moral truth based on his very nature and character. The Bible is the authoritative truth from God himself. And our task is to discover his truth within the pages of Scripture. And when we do understand what God is saying to us we are to personally apply that truth to life.

## WRITTEN WITH PURPOSE

Each book of the Bible has an intended meaning. God wants us to discover that meaning. He wants to reveal himself and his truth within the text so that we might experience him—know and love him, live in his ways, and love those around us as he loves us. So essentially, our task is to interpret the words in order to understand their intended meaning.

To interpret is to draw out the true meaning of something written or spoken. We don't create the meaning; we are to simply interpret the original intended meaning. The apostle Peter tells us that "no prophecy of Scripture is a matter of one's own interpretation" (2 Peter 1:20 NASB). So rather than reading into a text what we think is correct we must draw out the meaning that God intends for us to understand. That process is called *exegesis*.

Exegesis is from the Greek word *exegeomai,* which means "to make known, to unfold in teaching, to declare by making known." The word is used in the Gospel of John, when the apostle says that Jesus "has *revealed* God to us" (John 1:18). The New American Standard Bible translates *exegeomai* as "He has *explained* him" (verse 18).

To properly interpret or explain and reveal the meaning of a passage of Scripture we engage in the process of exegesis. We do this by asking our probing questions of who, what, where, when, why, and how. And in the process we

1. examine the text to understand its grammatical construction;

2. seek to understand the meaning of individual words— literally, figuratively, culturally, and so on;

3. discover the historical context, such as the identity of the author, cultural setting, timeframe, and so on;

4. examine the message within the context of paragraphs, chapters, individual books, and the entire scope of scriptural truth; and

5. understand the timeless truth applied to those it was written to at the time and understand how that timeless truth applies to us today.

You will recall we used many, if not all, of these elements as we explained (exegeted) passages about the Samaritan woman, Mary, Peter, and so on. This process of interpreting the intended meaning of Scripture is critical if we are to experience the real God of the Bible.

Remember, because we are sinners by birth we carry a lot of baggage. And even after God has redeemed us, our perception is often dim and foggy and we are liable to misinterpret Scripture. There also exist in our world those who claim to be godly teachers but twist and distort scriptures from their intended purpose and add even more confusion. Paul's warning to the church at Corinth against false teachers is very relevant today because there are many who are "disguising themselves as apostles of Christ. But I am not surprised! Even Satan can disguise himself as an angel of light" (2 Corinthians 11:13-14 NLT).

That is why it is crucial for us to heed the challenge of Paul to "be diligent…[in] accurately handling the word of truth" (2 Timothy 2:15 NASB). This may at first glance seem like a daunting challenge. But it is not if we follow a proven process of determining the meaning of the Bible. Additionally, there are valuable study and reference tools that will aid us in the process that we will cover in the next chapter. But for now let's look at two key elements involved in the interpreting process: the *meaning of words* and the *context of those words*.

## THE MEANING OF THE WORDS

Language is composed of words, of course. Words are the building blocks of ideas. And when we assemble words together in sentences and paragraphs they become the basic unit of communication. This is true of any literary work. And the Bible is a literary work of words, sentences, and paragraphs that communicate God's truth to us, the truth that is applied to life through the person of the Holy Spirit.

But how we interpret those words is important because words change their meaning as they are associated with other words and phrases. So are the words of the Bible to be interpreted literally, figuratively, or what? And this is where understanding the use of metaphors and grammar comes in. Take, for example, Jesus' statement in John 6:35. Look up that passage and read verse 35.

*Metaphor*: What did Jesus mean when he said he was the "bread of life"? Part of interpretation is applying common sense, rather than taking words literally. We can understand passages better if we allow language to speak in ordinary ways, instead of imposing some kind of special, artificial standard for language usage in the Bible. As we said, the Bible is literature, and the same linguistic principles apply to it as to other writings. This means we cannot take every word of the Bible as literal. While we are correct to believe the Bible is true, we must allow metaphors, similes, and analogies to be what they are, and not force them to be literal.

For example, when Jesus says, "I am the bread of life," does he mean that he is a loaf of ground grain mixed with yeast and baked? If not, then what does he mean? He is saying metaphorically that he provides sustenance for our spiritual life, just as a loaf of bread provides sustenance for our physical life. This example is too obvious to question, of course. But you would be surprised at the contrived interpretations you hear when people try to make biblical metaphors read literally.

*Grammar*: In interpreting a passage we must not only look for metaphors, but also give attention to grammar. Grammar involves such things as verb tenses, questions, commands, subjects, and objects. These elements determine the structure of the language, and they are important factors in determining exactly what is being said.

---

When we properly understand grammar, as in this passage,
it helps reveal to us the true meaning—in this case the
eternal nature of Jesus and his oneness with God.

---

For example, grammar affects the interpretation of Jesus' statement "I am the bread of life" in regard to the verb tense. So what tense did Jesus use in referring to himself as the bread of life—past, present, or future?

Jesus did not say, "I was the bread of life" or even "I will be the bread of life." Jesus used the present tense: "I am the bread of life." The use of *I am* indicates the unchanging, always-the-same, eternal nature of Christ. That is significant. But the "I am" also had significance to his Jewish audience, who was very familiar with the great "I Am" phrase. Take a moment now and read about a specific encounter in Exodus 3:14.

In the Exodus passage Moses had just encountered God in the burning bush. When Moses asked God for the name he should give Pharaoh when he asked who had sent Moses, notice how God answered. He said his name was "I Am." This use of the same term, "I Am," by Jesus was not lost on those who heard him. The accusation the Pharisees had made concerning Jesus was that he made himself equal with God. Jesus, however, *is* the great "I Am." And he said as much to the Pharisees. He is the God who always is—the eternal sustainer of the universe and the eternal sustainer of our own lives. And when we properly understand grammar, as in this passage, it helps reveal to us the true meaning—in this case the eternal nature of Jesus and his oneness with God.

## THE MEANING OF THE WORDS WITHIN CONTEXT

Imagine you walk by me (Sean) as I'm talking to three or four of my friends. You overhear me say, "No, I'm leaving Stephanie next week. Scottie will stay with her." You don't stop to inquire further but step over to one of your friends. The following is what you could say.

"Did you hear the latest about Sean and Stephanie McDowell?" "No," your friend replies. "What?"

"I just overheard Sean say he's leaving her next week, and she's going to get custody of their boy."

Shocked and disappointed, your friend glances over toward me. "I can't believe it. There's another one of those Christian speakers who's always emphasizing relationship and can't live up to his own message. It's really a shame!"

What just happened? Did you accurately interpret my words? You would have heard me correctly because I did say I was leaving my wife next week and Scottie, our son, is staying with her. But what you didn't hear were the sentences before and after. Here are the words in context:

"I guess you're excited about the upcoming speaking tour in Israel," my friend says.

"Yeah, I'm really looking forward to it," I reply.

"You're leaving later this week, right? Is Stephanie going with you?" my friend inquires.

"No, I'm leaving Stephanie next week," I reply. "Scottie will stay with her." I pause. "I'll only be gone a week so it won't be too hard on us. I really hate being away from the family."

The point is, we can miss the true meaning of what is said or written when we take words out of context.

### Literary Context

Context is important to exegete a passage. This is often done by understanding the setting of a passage—what comes immediately before a verse and what comes after. Whether we isolate a statement like "I'm leaving Stephanie" or a Scripture passage and fail to interpret it within the whole of the narrative, we are in danger of misinterpreting its meaning.

To correctly draw the meaning from a text we must see it within its literary context. Remember when I (Josh) stated that I struggled with understanding Galatians 6:2? It wasn't that I misread "bear one another's burdens," it was that I was not seeing it within context. When I read three verses down and examined the Greek words for "burden" and "load" I was able to understand verse 2 within context of the whole passage.

When we read a passage out of context we are in danger of reading another meaning into the text that simply isn't there. Scholars call this *eisegesis*, which means "to read into." Most errors of interpretation come from reading into Scripture a meaning that just isn't there. And much of that can be avoided by reading the text within context. But we need to see more than a few verses before and after a biblical truth to interpret it within context. We need to see it within the context of the chapter and in fact the entire Bible. And that is where cross-referencing comes in.

## Cross-Referencing

Cross-referencing simply means the process of following a topic or a word from one verse to another within the Bible to discover all the book has to say on the subject. The power of cross-referencing is in the authority that is consulted. Since we are allowing Scripture to interpret Scripture, we can depend on the correctness of our findings.

Several resources are available to locate cross-references, and we will cover them in greater detail in the next chapter. For now we will limit our cross-referencing discussion to what you see in many versions of the Bible. They have cross-references listed in a separate column beside the verse. Your Bible may also have a concordance, which is another cross-referencing aid. Another useful tool is a chain-reference Bible. (The original such Bible, still available today, is the *Thompson Chain Reference Bible*.) A chain-reference Bible has elaborate marginal references and a reference index that helps you trace a given topic throughout the entire Scriptures.

Notice when we were discussing the present tense usage of "I am," we referred to Moses and the burning bush. How did we know the "I am" name was mentioned in Exodus 3:14? The cross-reference margin in our Bible referred us to the Exodus passage. In fact, in relation to just the words "I am," we find ten cross-references within the book of John listed in our Bible. Following those will provide a significant context to Jesus' saying, "I am the bread of life." But for now let's just stay within the context of John chapter 6 to examine the literary context of the passage. Take a few minutes and read the entire chapter. What do you find?

As you read the chapter you no doubt discovered that it centers entirely around Jesus being our sustaining life. It opens with a crowd coming to hear Jesus and Jesus asking Philip, "Where can we buy bread and feed all the people?" (verse 5). Jesus performs a miracle by feeding over 5000 people with five loaves and two fishes. "I am the bread of life" is set within the context of hungry people being miraculously fed, Jesus walking on the water, and the crowd following him for the wrong reasons. Jesus said, "I tell you the truth, you want to be with me because I fed you, not because you understood the miraculous signs" (verse 26).

Jesus met hungry people at the point of their need. But he wanted to do more than address their physical need to eat. "Don't be so concerned about perishable things like food," he said. "Spend your energy seeking the eternal life that the Son of Man can give you…I am the living bread that came down from heaven. Anyone who eats this bread will live forever" (verses 27,51).

There is so much meaning relevant to each of us in Jesus' statement that he is the bread of life, but we can't really interpret that meaning accurately without reading it within context. We allow the Scripture, in a sense, to interpret itself. The Holy Spirit wants to reveal the truth of his Word to us personally as we understand the relevance of his truth spoken or written to its audience at the time. And one way we can do that is by reading the Bible within its literary context.

Historical Context

The Bible was written in various historical time periods. The attitudes, setting, lifestyle, and political structure of a certain time will affect our understanding of a passage. Therefore, in order to "explain or reveal" the meaning of Scripture we must see it within the cultural context of the day. Let's consider Jesus' statement "I am the bread of life" in its cultural context. What does that tell us about how to interpret it?

The historical setting was the first century during the Roman occupation of Israel. At that time bread was the main food source. It was not a supplement to the main meal as it is today—something to eat along with your steak, soup, or salad. Bread was the main meal. So Jesus' use of bread as the metaphor stresses his vital importance to the spiritual life of his hearers. Just as without bread they would die physically, without Jesus they would die spiritually.

When we read the Bible we are entering into the past. The Scriptures were written over a 1500-year span. Within that timeframe there were significant cultural, political, and sociological changes. As we understand the historical setting of when a specific passage was written we can better understand what God was saying to them and why. We will see the importance of cultural context more fully in the chapters to follow.

## REVIEWING THE INTERPRETIVE PROCESS

When you read the Bible, is your goal to understand what God is saying to you? Do you want to come to know him more deeply, know how you are loved by him, and how to love others like him so you can honor him and be blessed? To do so you and I, as we have discussed here, must understand what God meant when he inspired some 40 writers to pen his words. Then we can understand what God is saying to us now in the twenty-first century.

---

Even though the words of Scripture may not have been written specifically *to* us in the twenty-first century, it doesn't mean they weren't written *for* us.

---

This actually requires a two-step process that is to flow together as a blended process of interpreting God's Word. The first step is to determine what the passage meant for the ones who first spoke the words or wrote them down and what it meant to those who heard them or read them. That is when the historical setting becomes so important, as our previous examples have shown. Jesus, for example, was conveying something very important about himself and about a Samaritan woman when he talked with her at the well. By understanding what was said, who said it, how it was said, where it was said, when it was said, and why it was said—we learned something very revealing of who and what Jesus was like and the kind of relationship he wanted with the Samaritan woman. Grammar and word usage also gave us greater insight. And when we saw this meeting in the fuller context of Jesus' life, his mission, and God's overall plan for the human race we were able to more accurately interpret the passage.

The same can be said of our understanding of the passages about Peter and Mary. When we studied the words in the original language in Galatians 6 within context we also understood what it meant to "bear one another's burdens." All of our efforts were made to interpret what the meaning was to those Jesus or Paul spoke to.

In this first step we need to remember that nothing spoken or written in Scripture was spoken or written to us living in the twenty-first century. Jesus was speaking to his disciples, the crowds, and various individuals. When the apostles wrote the Gospels and Paul, Peter, James, and others wrote the books of the New Testament they had certain audiences in mind. It's unlikely they foresaw that some 2000 years later their writings would be published as the authoritative holy Bible for the entire human race. The point is, they wrote what they wrote within a historical context to audiences considerably different than those in the world today. But even though the words of Scripture may not have been written specifically *to* us in the twenty-first century, it doesn't mean they weren't written *for* us. However, because God was revealing himself and his truth to a specific audience within a specific time in history, our initial task is to interpret what he intended to communicate to them at the time.

However, then comes the next step: understanding what universal, relevant truth God is revealing to us right now. Remember the Bible is no ordinary literary work. It is the living Word from the living God. That Word is relevant to each person living today and is applicable to every situation in life, no matter what our cultural setting. The writer of Hebrews said,

> The word of God is full of living power. It is sharper than the sharpest knife cutting deep into our innermost thoughts and desires. It exposes us for what we really are. Nothing in all creation can hide from him. Everything is naked and exposed before his eyes. This is the God to whom we must explain all that we have done (Hebrews 4:12-13 NLT).

The truth of God's Word transcends history, cultures, customs, languages, and timelines. So when we are trying to understand what God wanted the people to know when he gave them his Word, we are also wanting to understand what he wants us to know today in our own lives—because the Scriptures are an ever-living document. We can "know these things," Paul wrote, "because God has revealed them to us by his Spirit, and the Spirit searches out everything and shows us even God's deep secrets" (1 Corinthians 2:10 NLT).

The apostle Paul goes on to say that he spoke with words given to him by the Spirit "using the Spirit's words to explain spiritual truths" (1 Corinthians 2:13). There are truths from the Old and New Testament that the Holy Spirit wants to apply to us. Our response can then be, "God, what do you intend for me to understand—to experience—from the passages I read and hear from your book? My heart is open. Help me to discover your intended message to me within the context of our loving relationship."

Experiencing God's Word in this way is a fascinating journey. It is an exciting discovery process of not only unlocking what God was revealing to his people thousands of years ago, but what he is revealing to you in your life, today. This underscores the need for the accurate exegesis of Scripture. You need to dig deep to discover the purpose he gave his words of truth so many years ago. Then he wants you to experience that truth now, with him. For Truth is a person, and he wants to empower you with his wisdom, love, and strength to face every challenge in life. "Then you will be filled with the fullness of life and power that comes from God" (Ephesians 3:19 NLT).

With the motivation to be empowered with wisdom, love, and strength to face all that life serves up, we move on to the tools of properly interpreting the Bible. We may want to know what God's Word means, but without the proper tools of discovery it will be difficult to uncover that meaning. This is the topic of the next chapter.

# Chapter 8

# Tools of Interpretation

*"I read my Bible, but I'm not sure I always properly interpret it.
What tools do I need to understand the real meaning of Scripture?"*

This is the question a lot of people have who want to really get into God's Word. Merely reading the Bible like you read a novel or non-fiction book is not enough. As we have stated earlier, to experience the Bible with its intended meaning we must pursue that meaning as if digging for buried treasure. And that requires some digging tools. Following is a list of the main tools that can greatly aid you in the process of interpreting God's Word. In the following chapters you will begin to put these tools to work.

## DEFINITIONS AND WORD STUDIES

The most effective way to interpret a word from the Bible—that is, to know the meaning of it—is to look it up in a dictionary. Usually a Bible dictionary will give you an expanded biblical definition of a word. A good Bible dictionary gives you not only the definition and the background of a word, but also its Old Testament and New Testament usages. Search the Internet for "Bible Dictionary" and you find sites that offer you free online services by which you can look up most words in the Bible. There you will also see a number of resources to purchase if you are seeking a hard-copy version of a Bible dictionary or software programs.

But why doesn't it suffice to simply look up a word in question in an English dictionary to get a clearer understanding? As you know, the Bible was not written in English. The New Testament was primarily written in Greek and the Old Testament in Hebrew. Often, to gain a clear understanding of a passage we must go back to the original language.

It is not that Greek or Hebrew is any more precise than English—it is that those who speak and write English simply express their thoughts differently. And when we know how a thought or concept in the Greek or Hebrew is being expressed we can then understand more clearly the intended meaning of the words.

A case in point. Let's say you purchased a car and you were having all kinds of mechanical problems with it. Finally in frustration you go to the owner of the car dealership to lodge your complaint. And to your surprise the owner says, "No worries—I'll simply give you another car. I'll call over to the service department and they will take care of you."

So, feeling gratified that your car troubles are over, you walk to the service department to get your replacement. But to your horror the replacement is a beat-up junker that is 20 years older than your own! You think, *When he said another car, I expected to get a car better than the one I have now!*

If your car dealer had spoken in the Greek language, you could have addressed this issue head-on even before seeing your replacement car. For example, the car dealer says to you, "No worries, I'll simply give you *allos* [another] car." *Allos* translated as "another" indicates numerical difference and denotes another *of the same sort*. But of course, you don't want just another car of the same sort, you want a qualitatively different car—a better car.

---

It's good when looking up words in dictionaries
to also check out their opposites, or antonyms.
Often opposites help define each other.

---

So you respond, "Thank you, but I don't want *allos* car, I would like *heteros* [another] car." *Heteros* denotes a qualitatively different car, or another *of a different sort.* You want a different and better car than you now have, and your use of the word *heteros* would make that clear.

The Greek language makes this distinguishing difference by using two separate words that both translate into English as the word "another." When speaking in English we have to use another set of words to make that distinction. When Jesus, for example, promised to send "another" comforter or counselor in the person of the Holy Spirit, what word for "another" did he use? He said *allos* counselor, which meant "another of the same sort," one like himself—not *heteros*. Jesus was assuring us that he would never leave us or forsake us because when we have the Holy Spirit it is like having Jesus with us.

You may see the value of such word studies, yet you don't know the Greek language and you think it is unrealistic that you will ever learn it. And that is where scholars like W.E. Vine have given us such valuable resources. Vine's *Expository Dictionary of New Testament Words* and *Expository Dictionary of Old Testament Words* provide us clear and precise meanings of the original words of Scripture.

There are also concordances with Hebrew and Greek lexicons that also give meanings of the original language of Scripture. One of the most widely used is Strong's Concordance. Search "Greek Dictionary" online and you will find a variety of resources in print, online, and in software programs. Also check with your local Christian bookstore.

It's good when looking up words in dictionaries to also check out their opposites, or antonyms. Often opposites help define each other. For example, when looking up "love," also look up "hate." It is helpful to look up related words as well. For instance, when looking up "Pharisees," also look up "Sadducees." When looking up "Teacher," also look up "Education," and even "Jewish Education." Following such trails will both expand and sharpen your knowledge of a subject.

## BIBLE TRANSLATIONS AND PARAPHRASES

The next resource to consider is translations of the Bible. There are over 20 English translations of the Bible on the market. Go to Bible gateway.com and click on available versions. You can then check out how each version varies and their features.

We offer one word of caution about the use of paraphrases. Paraphrases are often done by one person, and as good as they may be, they will inevitably reflect his or her viewpoint. For accurate interpretation always go to a good translation put together by a committee of respected scholars.

## REFERENCE BOOKS

Today many other resources are available for cross-referencing and looking up words, ideas, Bible history, and information about life, thinking, and attitudes in Bible times. We have already mentioned some of these book categories, but we will list a few of them again below. They include study Bibles, Bible encyclopedias, commentaries, and atlases. These materials give us the scholarly insights of experts and observations by people who have spent a lifetime of research and study into subjects we may never be able to explore for ourselves. Often such books can supply wide-ranging information that is immensely helpful in bringing understanding and clarity to Bible words or passages.

You may have encountered people who insist they will use nothing in their study but the Bible itself. They believe that if one is sufficiently "led by the Spirit," they will not need to depend on other books or insights from scholars or teachers to understand the Bible. The Bible itself refutes this thinking and makes it clear that God has given us teachers, as well as other Christians with specialized gifts designed to build up the church and strengthen members (see Romans 12, 1 Corinthians 12, and Ephesians 4:11-16). Over the centuries, like W.E. Vine and James Strong, many devout and dedicated Christians have compiled written resources that can be highly valuable to us in learning more about the truth of the Bible.

Here is a list of additional types of resources that you may find useful:

**Study Bibles.** A study Bible is one of the most useful study tools you can own. Many such Bibles contain wide-ranging information that you would have no way of knowing unless you were a Bible teacher or a serious student. A good study Bible may replace many of the types of reference books listed below. Many study Bibles include a brief Scripture commentary, introductions to books of the Bible and summaries of them, charts, maps, graphs, sidebars, textual footnotes, chain references, dictionaries, concordances, and other informational help that may often deflect the need to turn to other resources.

Most study Bibles are designed around a given theme. There are men's study Bibles, women's study Bibles, and application study Bibles, for example. Others are based on such things as prophecy, spiritual warfare, or evangelism. And new ones appear in the market regularly. I (Sean) personally saw the need for *The Apologetics Study Bible for Students* and teamed up with the publisher of the Holman Christian Standard Bible translation to produce it as general editor. Examine these different study Bibles for yourself and choose the one that best fits your needs and those of your family.

We have mentioned earlier that most study Bibles have the cross-referencing feature. For additional clarification let's examine how a study Bible cross-references a word.

In the *NLT Study Bible,* for example, we encounter the word "Pharisee" first in Matthew 3:7. An entire half a page is devoted to profiling the Pharisees, providing a brief definition of both Pharisees and Sadducees, along with an explanation of their origins and traditions. The margin then cross-references every verse in the Bible that contains the word "Pharisee." The subject index in the back of the study Bible breaks it down even further. It not only cross-references the word "Pharisee" but identifies the context in which the word is used, such as "belief and spiritual conditions of," "as believers in Jesus Christ," "Jesus Christ's conflict with," and so on. By following these cross-references we get a clear picture of who the Pharisees were, what they believed, and how they behaved. From these descriptions we see more clearly why they opposed Jesus so vehemently. Information we glean from a study Bible cross-referencing tool is invaluable to the interpretive process.

**Atlases.** A Bible atlas or even a general atlas is useful in helping us picture the movements and travels of Bible characters and peoples. For example, in exegeting John 4, where we're told that Jesus and his disciples left Judea and traveled through Samaria to get to Galilee, the atlas would help us to visualize their journey by showing us the relationship of the three geographical areas and the distance they had to travel. Atlases are also useful in showing the changes in political boundaries over the centuries. A map of Palestine at the time of its settlement by the 12 tribes of Israel is quite different from the same region under Roman occupation in the time of Christ. Atlases can show the scope of the great empires involved in Bible history—the Egyptian, Assyrian, Babylonian, Persian, Greek, and Roman. You can understand much more about Paul's hardships on his journeys if you study his travels on a map showing the Mediterranean region of the first century.

Sometimes a map may provide the essential key to unlocking our understanding of a Bible passage or book. We can hardly get a clear understanding of the book of Joshua, for example, without one. Only by referring to a map as we read of the conquest of Canaan can we appreciate the brilliance of Joshua's battle strategy. World War II general Douglas MacArthur and Israeli general Moshe Dayan both admired Joshua as a general and studied his plan for defeating the Canaanites. No doubt as these men read Joshua, they traced his military movements on good maps.

All study Bibles, and even many editions of the Bible, contain most of the maps you will need. However, some people want an atlas as an additional resource for more in-depth and detailed geographical information.

**Encyclopedias.** Both general encyclopedias, such as the *Encyclopedia Britannica*, and Bible encyclopedias are helpful research tools. They can give us broad information on Bible history, geography, culture, people, artifacts, and archaeology. Naturally, a Bible encyclopedia is more focused and detailed on Bible subjects than a general encyclopedia. Again, a good study Bible can provide much of what we will find in a Bible encyclopedia, though, of course, not with the same depth and detail.

**Commentaries.** A Bible commentary is exactly what the term implies. It is a Bible scholar's comments explaining the meaning of Bible passages.

Commentaries can be in-depth, verse-by-verse multivolume works or single-volume works on the entire Bible that treat the basic themes of chapters and hit certain highlighted verses. One staple feature of study Bibles is that they all have a running commentary accompanying the text.

Of course, any time we use a commentary, we must remember that we are reading the viewpoint of a single author. These authors are human and capable of erring just as we are. We must always have our senses alert to compare what commentaries teach with what we observe for ourselves in the Bible.

**Topical books.** Christian bookstores are filled with books on any topic you want to learn about in depth. You can buy scholarly or popularly written books on subjects like justification, redemption, salvation, sanctification, Christian living, God, the Holy Spirit, Jesus...you name it. If your focus in Bible study is a particular topic, check with your local bookstore or online for the best resources available.

## COMPUTER RESOURCES

Several times in this book we have referred to the resources both online and in software that can be installed on your own computer. Many of these computer resources can replace the books we listed above. An excellent example of an online resource is the one we've already mentioned, Biblegateway.com, which is superb for finding specific scriptures and linking references. By just typing in your Scripture reference or a word or two, you can use it as a concordance, or to look up the text of any verse in the Bible in any version. And with computer resources the response is immediate. Not only do you save the time of turning pages, you also save the time involved in writing the passage down. You can merely copy it and paste it into a document.

---

Such programs...have many visual features, including photos, illustrations, animated clips of many Bible incidents, and archaeological information.

---

If you obtain a Bible software program to install on your computer you can essentially get every book we've mentioned above. Such programs will have a Bible dictionary, a Bible encyclopedia, the complete text of the Bible in a number of versions with several ways of accessing them, cross-referencing tools, Bible-study helps, charts, maps, and commentaries. In addition they have many visual features, including photos, illustrations, animated clips of many Bible incidents, and archaeological information.

There are a number of Bible software programs such as Logos Bible, Biblesoft, BibleWorks, iLumina, and others. Check these out online or contact your local Christian bookstore.

## ORGANIZING WHAT YOU INTERPRET

For many years I (Josh) have used charts to aid me in the interpreting process. This is nothing more than a way to organize what I am discovering in Scripture. You can accomplish the same thing through extensive note-taking. But I have preferred to organize my notes in the form of charts.

There are four charts we will cover here, and then you will have the opportunity to create these for yourself as you are guided through a book of the Bible in chapter 10. In chapter 9 we will demonstrate the use of one of these charts. Following are descriptions and examples of each chart.

**Observation Chart:** This is a chart that notes the Scripture passage you are studying, the questions you are asking, and your observations about the passage (see below). This is simply a means to chronicle and organize what you are discovering as you read your Bible. It is especially helpful when you are cross-referencing Scripture passages.

| OBSERVATION CHART—EXAMPLE | | |
|---|---|---|
| Scripture | Questions | Observations |
| | | |

**Title Chart:** This chart is designed to give you the big picture of a chapter or an entire book of the Bible. It also helps you instantly recall what the book is about. In fact, we have found a Title Chart helps fix the content of a book clearly in your mind without the special effort of memorizing (see below).

As we have already noted, most Bible translations and all study Bibles chart out every book of the Bible by titling each chapter and providing paragraph titles. And this is what a Title Chart does. So the work is actually done for you with these translations. The basic advantage of creating a Title Chart of your own is to see a chapter or entire book of the Bible in one snapshot. If you are creating your own titles, it organizes them. It is also helpful if you are leading a Bible study to have a ready access of a snapshot overview.

| TITLE CHART—EXAMPLE | | |
|---|---|---|
| Chapters | Chapter 1 | Chapter 2 |
| Chapter title | | |
| Paragraph titles | | |
| Key verse(s) | | |
| Key word | | |

**Interpretation Chart:** This chart is to record what the passage reveals about its intended meaning, its meaning applied to you, and how you plan to experience or have experienced the passage. Again, writing this out in a chart helps solidify what you have discovered in your heart and mind. It also guides you in sharing with others the biblical truths you are experiencing (see below).

| INTERPRETATION CHART—EXAMPLE | |
| --- | --- |
| Intended meaning | |
| Meaning applied to me | |
| Experiencing the passage | |

**Outline Chart:** The outline chart differs from the Title Chart in that it allows you to expand and go deeper into the explanation of a passage, chapter, or even an entire book. The Outline Chart enables you to record the theme of a chapter, for example, and then break that down into sections, sub-sections, and notations under the sub-sections (see below).

| OUTLINE CHART—EXAMPLE #4 |
|---|
| I. |
|    A. |
|       1. |
|       2. |
|    B. |
|       1. |
|       2. |
|    C. |
| II. |
|    A. |
|    B. |
|       1. |
|       2. |
| III. |
|    A. |
|       1. |
|       2. |
|          a. |
|          b. |
|    B. |
|       1. |
|       2. |

```
IV.
  A.
  B.
  C.
  D.
```

Whether you elect to use a chart method or extensive note-taking, the key is to find a way to organize what you discover in a passage and crystallize it in a manner that makes sense to you. In cross-referencing passages, for example, you need some forum to record your findings. The Observation Chart can help you do that. The following is an exercise in using such a chart. As you recall, cross-referencing is an important step in the process of understanding a passage of Scripture within context.

## AN EXERCISE: INTERPRETING MATTHEW 7:1 IN CONTEXT THROUGH CROSS-REFERENCING

Read Matthew 7:1. By reading this one verse, would you think that Jesus is commanding his disciples not to judge others? On the surface it would appear so. And many people have used this verse to say that we are prohibited to judge others. However, this verse is one of the most commonly misused verses in the Bible. Yet through the simple process of cross-referencing, this statement of Jesus is placed within context, and we are able to understand his meaning.

I (Josh) wrote an e-book following the 9/11 disaster entitled *Know Good from Evil*. The e-book largely dealt with why we as a culture feel we do not have the right to judge others. Drawing from that material, let's answer some questions together and cross-reference other Scripture passages to get answers.

Context is vital. Who was Jesus speaking to when he said, "Do not judge others"? What was the setting?

_____

_____

_____

Matthew 7:1 is part of Jesus' Sermon on the Mount, which is recorded beginning in Matthew chapter 5.

How did Jesus begin his Sermon on the Mount? What was he calling people to do, and what were his teachings about?

_____

_____

Jesus' sermon begins with a statement about those who enter the kingdom of God (Matthew 5:3). Jesus is continually calling people to the kingdom throughout his sermon. So any interpretation of what he said needs to be set within the context of his kingdom message. Given that context, Jesus is presenting an ethic to his disciples to follow. He is sharing his kingdom view of how to think, be, and live in this world—his worldview. And in this passage he says for us not to judge.

Then if we are not to judge, who has the right to judge and why? Read Deuteronomy 32:35 and Leviticus 19:18.

_____

_____

_____

Again, the context is Jesus ushering his kingdom in, with him as the Righteous King, the Perfect Standard, the Judge of all. God proclaimed, "It is mine to avenge; I will repay" (Deuteronomy 32:35 NIV). He told Israel to "not seek revenge or bear a grudge" (Leviticus 19:18). Why? Because judgment belongs to the Righteous Judge. When a person condemns another he or she in effect presumes to determine who can and cannot be forgiven by God. And in doing so would usurp his rightful position as Judge.

Does this mean then we must abandon our moral sensibilities as Christ-followers and take no moral stand? If so, why or why not? Read Matthew 7:2.

_____

_____

_____

Listen to what Jesus says next. "The standard you use in judging is the standard by which you will be judged" (Matthew 7:2). So now it is becoming clear that we are to judge, but we must be careful which standard of judgment we use. It is not our standard of judgment, but his that is to do the judging.

When is it permissible to judge? To make godly judgment, what must first happen within us? Read Matthew 7:4-5 and Leviticus 19:17.

_____

_____

_____

_____

Jesus goes on to explain about those who worry about a speck in another person's eye when they have a log in theirs. He asks, "How can you think of saying to your friend, 'Let me help you get rid of that speck in your eye,' when you can't see past the log in your own eye? Hypocrite! First get rid of the log in your own eye, then you will see well enough to deal with the speck in your friend's eye" (Matthew 7:4-5).

Jesus was not directing his disciples to never judge others—he was emphasizing that their first responsibility was to purify themselves. When God first gave his instructions to Israel he said, "Do not nurse hatred in your heart...[yet] confront people directly so you will not be held guilty for their sin" (Leviticus 19:17). This suggests that it is not wrong to judge and confront the wrong being done; rather, it is wrong to judge while hypocritically harboring ill will toward others and overlooking sin in our own lives.

God is the righteous Judge. He establishes the standard for judging, not us. Yet he expects his followers to judge rightly. By additional cross-referencing we notice 19 places we are to make judgments. This is our Observation Chart, which asks one question—"What does this passage say about making judgments about issues or people?" Read the following Scripture verses and make your own observations. Then compare them with ours.

| SCRIPTURE | OBSERVATION |
|---|---|
| Matthew 7:15-20 | Jesus commands his disciples to make a judgment about individuals who claim to be God's prophets. |
| Matthew 10:11-15 | When Jesus sends his disciples on an evangelistic mission, he instructs them to make a judgment about the households in the towns. |
| Matthew 16:6-12 | Jesus tells his disciples to make a judgment about the teachings of the Pharisees and Sadducees and to beware of their teaching. |
| Matthew 18:15-17 | Jesus instructs his disciples to take appropriate action when a disciple is involved in sin. In order to carry out this action, it is necessary to determine what constitutes sin. |
| John 7:24 | Jesus tells the Jewish leaders to "stop judging by mere appearances, and make a right judgment" (NIV). Jesus does not forbid the act of judging but rather insists that it be exercised without hypocrisy, based on reality, and grounded in spiritual discernment. |
| Acts 5:1-10 | Peter makes a judgment against Ananias and Sapphira. |

| Romans 2:1 | Paul says we condemn ourselves if we pass judgment on another for doing the same things we do ourselves. Condemnation results from judging hypocritically. |
|---|---|
| Romans 14 | While Paul forbids believers to judge one another concerning matters of Christian liberty, he also exhorts believers to make informed choices. This passage shows how the prohibition against judgment and the admonition to judge can exist simultaneously. |
| 1 Corinthians 5:5 | Paul commands the Corinthian church to make a judgment concerning the sinning believer. |
| Galatians 1:8-9 | Paul makes a strong judgment against those who distort the gospel message and asks the Galatians to do the same. |
| Philippians 3:2 | Paul instructs the Philippians to watch out for evil men. |
| 2 Thessalonians 3:14 | Paul instructs the Thessalonians to take special note of undisciplined meddlers and to avoid associating with them. |
| 2 Timothy 3:1-9 | Paul describes the wickedness of certain people and instructs Timothy to have nothing to do with them. |

| | |
|---|---|
| 2 Timothy 4:2,14-15 | Paul tells Timothy that his proclamation of God's Word must involve reproof. Paul makes an implicit judgment in verses 14-15, where he identifies Alexander the metalworker as being opposed to the gospel. |
| James 4:11 | James provides a prohibition against judging that is very similar to Matthew 7:1. It may, in fact, be dependent upon Jesus' words given in the Sermon on the Mount. |
| 2 Peter 3:16-17 | Peter describes individuals who are ignorant and unstable, and who distort the Scriptures to their own destruction. These individuals scoff at the Lord's return and the coming judgment. |
| 1 John 4:1-3 | John instructs the church to test whether a prophet is true or false. |
| 3 John 1:9-11 | John addresses the pride and gossip of Diotrephes and says that he will confront Diotrephes when he arrives. |
| Jude | Jude warns the church that there are godless, immoral men who have slipped into the church without the believers' awareness. The church is to contend for the faith and not allow such men to corrupt it with false teachings and wicked practices. |

## INTERPRETING THE MEANING OF MATTHEW 7:1

Based on the cross-referencing we have done here together, what is Jesus' meaning, within context, when he said, "Do not judge others, and you will not be judged" (Matthew 7:1)?

_____

_____

_____

_____

_____

_____

Through the cross-references in Scripture regarding the judging of others it becomes clear that judging is quite permissible. What is prohibited is judging the wrong way. We are not to judge according to our own preferences, for it is God who ultimately judges us all. We are to uphold his standards. We are not to judge while hypocritically overlooking our own sins but to assess others and ourselves with honesty. We are to see things as God sees things. We are not to become dull in our moral discernment, for not everyone values his standard of truth. When we understand these things, we realize that proper judging is not only allowed; it is our obligation as a follower of Christ.

## TAKE THE NEXT STEP

This is but one example of how using the one simple tool of cross-referencing can help us interpret the meaning of Scripture. And a discovery of this nature can of course lead us to a deeper knowledge and love for God and a clearer understanding of how we are to live in relationship with others. But there is yet another use of our truth discovery—sharing it with others. In the next chapter we will review the steps to unlocking the truths of the Bible and explain how to outline a passage so you can effectively share it with others.

# Chapter 9

# Sharing Your Insights with Others

**B**lind from birth, yet he sees. Bent and buckled limbs, but now he walks. Lepers as outcasts of society are now cleansed. When Jesus' miraculous touch healed those who were sick, or when he fed the hungry or forgave the sinner's debt, one common theme stands out—the healed ones wanted to tell others.

---

*When you impart what you are learning on your journey into Scripture, you are actually participating in Christ's mission to build his kingdom.*

---

When you have experienced something extraordinary, it is natural to want to tell others. And when it comes to gaining a fresh insight into God's truth there is nothing more thrilling than to watch others impacted by what you share. Jesus actually planned it that way. He told his disciples, "You must also tell others about me because you have been with me from the beginning" (John 15:27 NLT). He prayed to his Father, "As you sent me into the world, I am sending them into the world" (John 17:18).

What you discover in Scripture is meant to be passed on to others. God wants to share his life and truth through you to others. When you impart what you are learning on your journey into Scripture, you are actually participating in Christ's mission to build his kingdom. And that is truly an exciting mission to be on.

To effectively share what you have learned and experienced in Scripture, however, does require some forethought. You will need to assemble your insights into a form that makes them transferable. And you began that process through note-taking or by creating the various charts we have discussed in the previous chapter. That ultimately leads to creating a Passage Outline and the interpretation of that passage. Here in this chapter we will review the step-by-step process of Bible interpretation we have already touched on and then illustrate the creation of an Outline Chart.

## A 7-STEP PROCESS

These steps are not exhaustive, but they are what we consider the most basic in interpreting Scripture so you can pass on your discoveries to others.

### 1. Read the Book

Obviously you need to decide what portion of Scripture you are going to study and experience. As we indicated earlier, a person needs to study an entire book to gain full context of the passages within it. And multiple readings of the book are necessary to discover the many truths within it.

### 2. Read About the Book

Knowing about the book provides valuable context for your journey through it. A study Bible or Bible handbook will give you this valuable information. You will find such things about the book as

- a timeline;
- an introduction;
- its "vital statistics," including its purpose, the author, to whom it was written, the date written, the setting, the key verses, key places, key people, and other special features;
- its "megathemes";
- a map showing the locations of its key events.

### 3. Ask Questions and Record Your Answers

Using the six questions—who, what, where, when, why, and how—will allow you to probe the book to uncover its meaning. During this process you are first observing all that is going on to grasp the big picture of the book. As you continue to probe you drill down deeper and deeper, all the while recording your answers.

As you ask questions of a book, be aware of what is called "interconnecting questions." These add another dimension to your search by helping you examine how terms, people, places, or ideas in a passage or book interconnect with those of other passages. Ask questions like

a. *What things are alike or similar?*

This question is designed to help us look for similarities in a passage.

b. *What things are different?*

With this question, we do the opposite of what the first question asks. We look for contrasts rather than similarities.

c. *What things are repeated?*

Here we watch for repetition and, when we find things that are repeated, we ask why.

d. *What evidence of cause and effect do we see?*

Cause and effect means that one things leads to another. Sometimes passages containing cause and effect don't necessarily jump out at us, but certain words give us a clue. Words that link cause to effect are *because, for, therefore,* and *since.*

e. *What movement from the general to the specific do we see?*

This kind of movement happens often in Scripture. Notice in John it says, "He [Christ] came into the very world he created, but the world didn't recognize him" (John 1:10). Then in verse 11 it says, "He came to his own people [Israel], and even they rejected him." The first general statement sets up the second specific one. Look for the "general to the specific" movements in a passage.

f. *What progressions are evident?*

Here we look for an idea or an event building, developing, or unfolding. Often the progression will climax in a specific act or idea.

g. *What questions or answers are given?*

Questions and answers often carry arguments that culminate in providing us insight. Jesus often used questions to make a point. Questions many times serve to emphasize the truth of God's Word.

h. *What problems and solutions are presented?*

Problems presented and solutions offered often capture important insights into the meaning of Scripture.

i. *What commands and promises do we see?*

Look for commands that are the boundaries God has given us to follow and observe the promises or blessing in obeying those commands. Such obedience deepens our relationship with God.

j. *What relational meaning do we see?*

As we stated above, even commands have a relational meaning. The whole of Scripture is given within the context of relationships. And God wants us to understand that relational meaning so we can enjoy a deepened relationship with him and one another.

## 4. Unlock the Meaning of Words

As we have mentioned, the Hebrew and Greek languages are rich in meanings that the English translations don't always reflect. Using a dictionary or lexicon to gain a deeper and clearer understanding of a verse is important. However, care must be taken to accurately translate words from the original to English. This is where Bible word-study resources written by language scholars and theologians become critical.

## 5. Interpret the Intended Meaning of the Text

Our goal in examining a passage or a book is to accurately exegete—explain its intended meaning. We have covered this point extensively in chapters 7 and 8. The one thing we would add here is the importance of comparing our findings with the historical body of church doctrines and writings. If, for example, you come up with an interpretation of a passage contrary to fundamental doctrines of the church—beware!

---

We are wise to read and learn from the ancient church fathers and more recent orthodox writers to know what is considered the foundational building blocks of the true faith.

---

By the third century the church had identified the core doctrines of Christianity (see the Nicene Creed on page 36), and for the most part those same core doctrines have been the central interpretation of Scripture down through the centuries. Of course there have been disagreements and varied views on a number of the particulars. Yet there is a vast body of believers today who still unite around the core issues of the early church, such as the reliability and authority of Scripture, original sin, Christ's deity, Christ's atonement, justification through faith, Christ's bodily resurrection, the Trinity, and so on. So we are wise to read and learn from the ancient church fathers and more recent orthodox writers to know what is considered the foundational building blocks of the true faith, and hold to them.

## 6. Experience the Relational Meaning of the Text

God gave us his Word because he wants an intimate, loving relationship with us. He wants us to equally enjoy a loving relationship with one another, and he wants to extend his kingdom and his relationship with us into eternity. So to read his Book and not experience its relational meaning would be to misinterpret the very reason he gave it to us.

Our first priority is to understand who each book was originally written to and its intended meaning. But then we are to quickly move on to experience its relational meaning personally and corporately as a church.

The following questions will help guide you to apply the relational meaning with God and others:

- How does this scripture relate to loving God more deeply with all my heart, soul, and mind?

- How does this scripture relate to loving others as God loves me?

- How does this passage reveal a fresh understanding of who God is?

- What about God's heart and motives do I see in this passage?

- What about God's plans and purpose do I see that relates to me in this passage?

- How does God see people differently than I do?

- How does my heart respond to this relational God, including his loving discipline?

- How does God want me to respond to those who are lost and without him?

## 7. Outlining a Passage or Book of the Bible

Once you have made extensive notes or gone through the process of filling out your charts, you are ready to create an outline of a passage or book. Again, the reason an outline is important is that it enables you to recall the scriptural insights you discovered and provides a systematic way or process of sharing your insights with others.

You will be given an opportunity to outline a book of the Bible in the next chapter. You can then make use of Observation, Title, and Interpretation Charts during that process. What your note-taking and recording does is enable you to eventually create a cohesive, easy-to-follow outline of the book. Following is an example of outlining the first 18 verses of the book of John.

## AN EXAMPLE OF OUTLINING

One way to determine what to outline is to go by the section divisions the publishers of the Bible you are using have placed within each chapter. This method gives you a head start, because these sections already have headings. A section division may incorporate two or more paragraphs. So what you are doing is identifying the major thoughts within a chapter.

You may also choose to add subdivisions to your passage outline. These subdivisions, for example, could be of words within the passage that have enough significance to warrant further exploration and study. This type of outlining will be especially useful as you share your insights with others. As we progress through this chapter you will see a sample outline of John 1:1-18 take shape.

The process of outlining is not as hard as you may think. In fact the passage itself will dictate to you the points of an outline. Those points should develop along the natural progression of the passage. You will want to avoid forcing into an outline a topic that you do not find within the passage, either explicitly or implicitly. As you construct your outline, you will want to constantly refer back to your notes or Observation Chart.

Now take a moment to read John 1:1-18. Feel free to take notes of what you find. Once you have read and made notes, compare your finding with the outline process we are about to follow.

In reviewing the notes and charts from our reading of John 1:1-18, we found four major points that emerged from this passage. Our first point comes from the observations of verses 1-5, in which we noted that these verses identify Christ as the Word who was God and was with God from the beginning, and who created the world. So, on our outline we place as our first heading **"The Word—The Uncreated Creator."** For our next heading, we use our observation about John the Baptist from verses 6-8: **"Forerunner of the Word."** Our third major division comes from verses 9-13: **"Results of the Word Made Flesh."** Then our fourth and last division is verses 14-18, which produces the heading **"Characteristics of the Word Made Flesh."** You can see our entire outline on the following page.

We consulted our notes and created subdivisions under these four major divisions. Under the first major division we found material for three subdivisions.

I. The Word—The Uncreated Creator (John 1:1-5)

A. Eternal existence

B. Eternal source

C. Eternal manifestation

Now we look for topics in our notes and charts that logically should be placed beneath these subdivisions. We sensed that Christ's divine nature fit logically beneath "Eternal existence," so we place it there. For item B, "Eternal source," our notes revealed that Christ was the source of everything made as well as of life itself. So under the subheading "B. Eternal source," we placed "Material world" and "Life." We didn't note additional material for "Eternal manifestation," so we left that topic without subdivisions.

Next we looked at the second major division of the passage, "Forerunner of the Word." We consulted our notes and charts and found information that would go under this title. Here a question prompted the answer we needed: "Who was the forerunner of the Word?" We had noted the answer from verse 6: The forerunner was John the Baptist, a man sent by God. So on our outline as the first subtopic under "II. Forerunner of the Word," we wrote, "A. John the Baptist: Man sent by God."

| **OUTLINE CHART SAMPLE** |
| --- |
| Witness of the Word Made Flesh |
| (John 1:1-18) |
| I. The Word—The Uncreated Creator (1-5) |
|   A. Eternal existence (1-2) |
|     1. Divine nature (1) |
|     2. Since the beginning (2) |
|   B. Eternal source of creation (2-4) |

1. Material world (3)
2. Life (4)

C. Eternal manifestation (light) (5)

II. Forerunner of the Word (6-8)

A. Who? Man sent by God (6)

B. Purpose? (7-8)

1. Bear witness of the light (7a, 8)
2. For all the world to believe (7b)

III. Results of the Word Made Flesh (9-13)

A. Negative (9-11)

1. Enlightens every man (9) BUT
2. Rejected by men (10-11)

a. by world (10
b. by his own (11)

B. Positive (12-13)

1. Children of God by believing (12)
2. Of God, not man (13)

IV. Characteristics of the Word Made Flesh

A. Only begotten of the Father (14)

B. Greater rank than forerunner (15)

C. Channel of grace and truth (16-17)

D. Visible expression of invisible God (18)

Next we asked why. Why was John sent by God? The question addresses the purpose of John's mission. So on our outline, as the second subtopic under "Forerunner of the Word," we wrote, "B. Purpose." We continued to consult our notes and charts for further information and answers, and we found two entries that explained John's purpose, in verses 7 and 8. "He came to bear witness of the light," and "for all the world to believe." So we entered these two items on our outline as subtopics 1 and 2 under "Purpose."

That is probably enough to give you the idea. Again, refer to the "Outline Chart Sample" and see how we outlined this passage. The important thing to remember when you are outlining is begin with the big idea; then you can divide that idea into subtopics found in your notes, Observation Chart, and Title Chart.

## IN SHARING WITH OTHERS: LEAD RATHER THAN TELL

My son, Scottie, and I (Sean) were walking along the beach one sunny afternoon. He was a few yards ahead of me. Suddenly he reached down to pick up something, turned, and ran back to me yelling, "Dad, look what I found!"

---

> You can walk your friends down the same discovery path you have gone. Lead them to ask the questions, discover answers, and piece together experiential insights into the meaning of the Bible.

---

As he approached he was waving a dollar bill in his hand. You would have thought by his excitement he had found a gold Spanish doubloon. He was beside himself. He kept saying, "I found a dollar—it was lying right there and I found it."

I could have given Scottie a dollar that day—I had done that many times before. But it would not have been the same. Why? Because Scottie had found the money himself.

It is the same with experiencing biblical truth. You can tell people about your own truth discovery, and that can truly impact their lives. But when you lead a person to discover a fresh insight for themselves— that is truly special. Because experiencing the Bible isn't a secondhand process; it is a personal encounter with the real God who wants each of us to discover him for ourselves.

We encourage you to share what you've experienced from Scripture with your family and friends. But if you want a special experience, ask a few friends to join you on a "Bible experience journey." Take a book of the Bible you have studied and experienced, like the one you are about to study in the next chapter. And then host an hour-a-week study with your friends. You can then walk them down the same discovery path you have gone. Lead them to ask the questions, discover answers, and piece together experiential insights into the meaning of the Bible. You will be greatly rewarded as they personally experience God's Word.

## EXPERIENCE THE BIBLE YOURSELF

Up to this point we have largely explained ways to experience the Bible, the process of interpreting passages, and the tools that are needed. Now we would like to shift gears and lead you to experience the Bible yourself.

The next two chapters guide you into the fascinating journey of the book of Hosea. This book provides one of the clearest big-picture views of the divine-human relationship in all of Scripture. Yet it has a profound meaning to each of us today. Some have found this journey to be God's transforming means to more deeply relate to him, his Book, and those around us. We pray that this scriptural journey will truly impact your life.

# Chapter 10

# "Go and Learn the Meaning of This Scripture"

It was another tough day at the table. Collecting taxes for the Romans was not easy. You had to have tough skin to do the job. Because it certainly didn't make you a popular person in town, especially if you were Jewish.

On this particular day, Jesus walked by a tax collector's table and saw a man named Matthew. "'Follow me and be my disciple,' Jesus said to him. So Matthew got up and followed him" (Matthew 9:9).

Later that day Matthew invited Jesus and his disciples to his place for dinner. He also invited others of his tax collector colleagues and other "disreputable sinners. But when the Pharisees saw this, they asked his disciples, 'Why does your teacher eat with such scum?'" (Matthew 9:10-11).

The Pharisees' response is understandable. Tax collectors were agents of the hated Roman government. So most Jews naturally resented paying the Romans, but they resented even more those Jews who did the Romans' bidding. So why would Jesus associate with those who worked for the oppressive Roman government? This was the very type of oppression from which the Messiah was supposed to deliver his people.

His disciples could have answered this way. "Well, Jesus is different. He welcomes all people and doesn't put anyone down for what they believe or what they do. We all need to be tolerant in today's world—you know, accept different views and get along with everyone. Don't you agree?"

Of course his disciples didn't respond that way to the Pharisees. It was Jesus himself that responded.

> When Jesus heard this, he said, "Healthy people don't need a doctor—sick people do." Then he added, "Now go and learn the meaning of this Scripture: 'I want you to show mercy, not offer sacrifices.' For I have come to call not those who think they are righteous, but those who know they are sinners" (Matthew 9:12-13).

Here Jesus tells the "learned" scholars of the day—the "experts" on the Hebrew text to "go and learn the meaning of this Scripture." Jesus had quoted from Hosea 6:6, a book the Pharisees were very familiar with. This obviously made them look foolish in front of everyone—which is a bit humorous. It probably felt a little rewarding for the disciples and the bystanders to watch Jesus confronting the Pharisees, who thought they knew it all. And in this situation he seemed to really put them in their place.

But what is the meaning of Hosea 6:6, which Jesus quoted? At first blush we might think that Jesus meant that we should care about people rather than worry about the law. But is that what this passage really means?

Jesus' very challenge "to go and learn the meaning" displays his insight. "Learn" in this passage is the Greek word *manthano*. This denotes learning by inquiry or observation. He was telling the Pharisees in effect that if they would dig deeper into Hosea 6:6, ask the right questions, and accurately observe what was going on there, they would understand why he was eating with sinners. Interestingly, Hosea was written to give the big-picture perspective on God's master plan for Israel and all of us. And of course Jesus was a very critical part of that plan. But the Pharisees couldn't see it. They didn't understand the meaning of Hosea.

This often overlooked and perhaps obscure book in the Old Testament does in fact provide a clear perspective of what God was up to with Israel and even with us today. And through observation—knowing what to look for by asking the right questions—we can learn the meaning of this passage. So as an exercise we would ask that you take time to read the entire book of Hosea and ask the "who, what, where, when, why, how" questions. We will provide a background of the book here, pose various questions that can serve as your template, and give you space to note what you discover. In the next chapter we will provide in-depth observations on the book of Hosea. You can then compare them with what you have experienced from your own discovery.

## THE BACKGROUND

The following has been gleaned from a Bible study and Bible handbook. We first ask: When was Hosea written and where? Who are the main characters? Why was the book written? Answering these questions gives us a context of the book.

Hosea was a prophet in ancient Israel. He wrote his book during the mid-700s BC. At the beginning of his time as a prophet, under the reign of King Jeroboam II, Israel expanded its borders, and some Israelites prospered greatly. After Jeroboam's death everything changed. In fact, three decades later, the Northern Kingdom—Israel—was destroyed by the Assyrian Empire.

The Northern Kingdom had been worshipping pagan gods, and during this tumultuous time the Israelites turned even more desperately to their pagan worship. They hoped their gods would save them from destruction. Hosea was the messenger of the true God. He warned of the coming destruction and offered Israel hope if they would only return to the God of Abraham, Isaac, and Jacob. But they would not.

God, of course, had made a covenant—a solemn promise—with Abraham over a thousand years before this. He said, "I will make a covenant with you, by which I will guarantee to give you countless descendants" (Genesis 17:2). He promised Abraham's descendants that they would be blessed and that he would be their loving covenant God of compassion and mercy. Moses told the children of Israel at Mount Sinai that God "did not set his heart on you and choose you because you were more numerous than other nations, for you were the smallest of all nations! Rather, it was simply that the LORD loves you, and he was keeping the oath he had sworn to your ancestors" (Deuteronomy 7:7-8).

---

"Concerning the Gentiles, God says in the prophecy of Hosea, 'Those who were not my people, I will now call my people. And I will love those whom I did not love before.'"

---

God wanted to powerfully illustrate the meaning of his commitment to Israel through Hosea. The main characters were Hosea and his wife, Gomer, and God and his children, the people of Israel. He chose marriage as the stage to unfold this profound living story of God and his wayward people—which is also applicable to us and the entire human race.

God made very specific promises to the children of Israel that will be literally fulfilled. And if you are not of the bloodline of Judah or any other Jewish tribe then certain promises He made to Israel don't apply to you. But if you have been made a child of God through Christ, then the apostle Paul makes it clear that you are clearly part of God's plan and his people. "And we are among those whom he selected, both from the Jews and from the Gentiles. Concerning the Gentiles, God says in the prophecy of Hosea, 'Those who were not my people, I will now call my people. And I will love those whom I did not love before.' And, 'Then, at the place where they were told, "You are not my people," there they will be called "children of the living God"'" (Romans 9:24-26). So while some of us may not be part of God's chosen people, Israel, we are still a part of God's called people, his church. With that as a background, take time now to read the 14 chapters of Hosea. When you are finished come back to this page and begin answering the questions. At the conclusion of this chapter we will ask you to interpret the passage Jesus quoted: Hosea 6:6.

## LEARN THE MEANING

Compare Matthew 9:13 and Hosea 6:6.

Jesus quotes Hosea 6:6. Fill in the word from Hosea 6:6: "I want

you to show _____." What is the Hebrew word used
here, and what does it mean?

_____

_____

_____


Review Hosea 1.

What did Hosea and Gomer name their children, what did their
names mean, and why was that significant?

_____

_____

_____


What kind of marriage was this, and why was it so dysfunctional?

_____

_____

_____


What is God's eventual plan regarding all this dysfunction?

_____

_____

_____


How does this family dysfunction (Hosea-Gomer and God-Israel)
relate to you? Are there times in your life that you can't quite feel God's
love either? Write out a prayer to God that addresses any of your own
dysfunctional relationships with God and others. Express your heart's
desire to him.

_____

_____

_____

_____

_____

Review Hosea 2, 6, and 7.

    Why is the wife unfaithful? What does she want—what is she looking for (chapter 2)?

_____

_____

_____

_____

Did Hosea provide her everything she needed (chapter 2)?

_____

God is a faithful provider, yet Israel was unfaithful to God—why? (See chapters 6–7.)

_____

_____

_____

_____

What lures you away from a committed love relationship with God, and why?

_____

_____

_____

_____

In what way are you prompted to trust God more? Write out your prayer response to God.

_____

_____

_____

_____

Review Hosea 11.

What does Israel's unfaithfulness cause God to feel?

_____

_____

_____

_____

How could God justifiably feel toward Israel, and what could he have done?

_____

_____

_____

_____

What could God justifiably do to you for your unfaithfulness, yet what has he done?

_____

_____

_____

_____

How does that make you feel—that God has shown you mercy rather than judgment? Write out your response to God here.

_____

_____

_____

_____

Review Hosea 2:4-5,9.

What does Hosea do (chapter 2) in response to Gomer's adultery, and why?

_____

_____

_____

_____

What does God do (chapter 9) in response to Israel's adultery, and why (chapter 5)?

_____

_____

_____

_____

Review Hosea 2 and 3.

What does it cost Hosea to get Gomer back (chapter 3)?

_____

_____

_____

_____

What did it cost God to get you back?

_____

_____

_____

_____

What kind of relationship do Gomer and Israel get when they return home (chapter 2)?

_____

_____

_____

_____

The God of *hesed* desires a deep, intimate husband-wife-type relationship with you. What does that prompt in you? Write out your response to God here.

_____

_____

_____

_____

Read Hosea 2:19-20. These verses were written to Israel but they are for you too, as well as for your family and friends. Summarize God's overarching desire for a lost and doomed human race.

_____

_____

_____

_____

Read Matthew 9:12-13 and Hosea 6:1-6. What is the meaning of Hosea 6:6 within the context of Jesus' response to the Pharisees? What was he saying to them about himself, about every fallen human who is not in relationship with him, and about those who do know God?

_____

_____

_____

_____

Now place yourself within the story of Hosea. What is God saying about you? What is your response to him?

_____

_____

_____

_____

_____

*ⱷⱷ*

In the next chapter we will walk through Hosea with you and provide an answer to each of the questions. The questions are actually answered by a Christian husband and father of two who sought the "meaning of the Scripture." His life and relationships were changed. Read on.

# Chapter 11

# Placing Yourself Within the Big Picture of Scripture

There it is, Planet Earth as seen from outer space. You are there capturing a picture of the entire globe surrounded by blackness with your camera lens. Then you begin to zoom in. As the world gets closer, North America fills the screen, then the United States, and then New England. Still your camera moves in until you are looking down on the distant buildings of a city. You move closer yet until you can see the streets with cars moving on them and people walking on the sidewalks. You aim your camera at a particular car, then the passenger window. Finally you zoom inside. You focus on the person driving the car. It is you!

You have probably seen that kind of fascinating zoom shot on TV. It's amazing how state-of-the-art computer technology can give us a single, seamless zoom shot that brings us from deep space to within a few inches of a person driving a car. And in one sense it illustrates the process you went through as you interpreted the book of Hosea. Because in that book we are able to discover the big picture of what the Bible is really all about. It tells the story of God's commitment to Israel, and that story is relevant to us today. Each of us fits within that story. Just like you have a specific place on Planet Earth where you live and a role you play in twenty-first-century life, you have a place and role in the sweeping story of Scripture.

In your own study of the book of Hosea you may have answered all the questions necessary to discover the meaning of Jesus' quote found in Matthew 9:13. But in this chapter we would like you to compare notes with someone else who has gone through the book of Hosea and specifically Hosea 6:6 to "learn the meaning of this Scripture."

His name is Dave. He is a Christian layperson in the church, a husband and father of two teenagers, and a computer software developer. Dave's journey is probably not unlike your own. He has read the Bible off and on during his Christian life, but he wanted to go beyond mere study to experience God and his Word more deeply. He has cultivated a heart of relational discovery and wants to know God more deeply.

Dave was hosting a Saturday-morning Bible study in his home with a handful of fellow believers from his church. They were studying the book of Matthew and of course came up to Matthew 9:13. Dave shared his subsequent journey through the book of Hosea with us, and we share it with you. As you read his observations and insights, compare them with your own.

## ONE MAN'S JOURNEY TO "LEARN THE MEANING"

I and five other men who had met at my home concluded our study that week. None of us felt certain we understood just what Jesus was getting at when he quoted Hosea 6:6 in Matthew 9, but we were moving on. Or so I thought.

---

"God…are you actually asking me to 'go learn the meaning of' Hosea 6:6 too? If so, what meaning do you want me to discover?"

---

During the week the words "go and learn the meaning of this Scripture" kept repeating themselves over and over in my head. I knew that Jesus was quoting the Greek translation of the Hebrew text (the Septuagint) of Hosea 6:6. So I read Matthew 9:13 and Hosea 6:6 in different translations. The New American Standard Bible translated Matthew 9:13 as "I desire compassion, and not sacrifice" and Hosea 6:6 as "I delight in loyalty rather than sacrifice."

I was curious why Matthew and Hosea used two different words.

They seemed to be different ideas to me. I checked out the New International Version and it used the word "mercy" in both passages. The New Living Translation said "show mercy" in Matthew and "show love" in Hosea. Here were four English words used for the same Hebrew word: love, compassion, mercy, and loyalty. *Which is the correct translation?* I wondered.

I looked up the Hebrew word and its literal translation. The word was *hesed*, meaning "loyal love, unfailing kindness, devotion, a love or affection that is steadfast based on a prior relationship." It now made sense why the four Bible translations rendered *hesed* differently. But I was somewhat confused. I wondered why Jesus would be quoting a passage about us having a committed love in regard to him eating with sinners. I clearly didn't have context. I was prompted to prayerfully ask, "God, what were you trying to get the Pharisees to understand from the book of Hosea? Are you actually asking me to 'go learn the meaning of' Hosea 6:6 too? If so, what meaning do you want me to discover?" With these questions motivating me, I began my journey into Hosea.

I was so captivated by what I was discovering week after week that I dug deeper and deeper. My journey lasted just over a year. The truth I discovered was to impact my view of God and his relationship with me, my relationship with my wife and my two children, my church relationships, how I saw the world, and my motivation to share with others. The Hosea experience gave me a new perspective on life and God's Word. And I have had a renewed motivation to "go learn the meaning of Scripture" ever since.

I began by reading the background notes on the book of Hosea in a Bible dictionary. I learned that God was using Hosea's relationship with Gomer as a powerful illustration of God's relationship with Israel. What I didn't expect is how powerful an illustration God would use in my own life. I began with asking central questions.

What kind of marriage is this?
Why such a dysfunctional family?

God told Hosea to do a strange thing. He instructed him to marry a prostitute who would be unfaithful to him. He was to take a bride who would go back to her prostituting ways. "This will illustrate how Israel has acted like a prostitute by turning against the LORD and worshipping other gods" (1:2).

So Hosea marries Gomer and has three children with her. The first child was a boy who God said to name Jezreel.

Jezreel was also the name of a valley in north central Israel where in 733 BC the Assyrian army defeated the Israelite forces and captured the area. The name *Jezreel* means "God plants." I found that this name depicts God scattering seed for a later harvest to grow. So this first child of Hosea and Gomer represents the hope of a meaningful harvest, a fruitful effort coming out of a soon-to-be-dysfunctional and disastrous marriage.

Their second child was a girl who God said to name *Lo-Ruhamah*, which means "not loved." And their third child was another boy, who God said to name *Lo-Ammi*, which means "not my people."

The very names of this couple's children were a foreshadowing of the dysfunctional family they would become. And more importantly, it represented the dysfunctional relationship between God and Israel.

God had great hopes and plans for Israel. They were his people, planted with the hope of a meaningful harvest. They were his Jezreel. "'I know the plans I have for you,' says the LORD. 'They are plans for good and not for disaster, to give you a future and a hope. In those days when you pray, I will listen. If you look for me wholeheartedly, you will find me'" (Jeremiah 29:11-13).

But Israel did not wholeheartedly look to the one true God, and disaster followed them repeatedly. They did not feel loved by God nor part of his family. Israel was both his Lo-Ruhamah and Lo-Ammi because Israel turned away from him. His hope of an intimate family relationship with his children was lost—but not forever.

As I read about this dysfunctional relationship between God and his people I prayed, "God, I know you have made me your child and that I am loved. I know I'm part of your family. But to be honest, at times I don't always feel your love either. The dysfunctional relationship with your chosen people far too often applies to me. And when it does I feel alienated and alone. I don't want that kind of relationship. I want to always feel your love."

Why is Gomer unfaithful?

What does she want?

It's obvious Hosea's wife becomes dissatisfied at home. Gomer says, "'I'll run after other lovers and sell myself to them for food and water, for clothing of wool and linen, and for olive oil and drinks'" (2:5). These are natural needs and it's normal to want them. But wasn't her husband meeting her needs? Wasn't the marriage fulfilling?

The reality is that Hosea was all that Gomer needed, but she didn't realize it. Hosea says, "She doesn't realize it was I who gave her everything she has—the grain, the new wine, the olive oil; I have even given her silver and gold" (2:8). Rather than focusing on the abundant love and provisions of her husband, Gomer was attracted to the flirtation of others. She leaves Hosea to sell her body, but she actually gets less in return than she had at home.

Israel did the same. God said, "Like Adam, you broke my covenant and betrayed my trust...[and] are all adulterers, always aflame with lust" (6:7; 7:4). This was the dysfunctional family history of God's people—God wanting to meet their every need, but they turn to their own ways and suffer for it. The children of Israel's King David did the same. David himself committed adultery with Bathsheba and then arranged the death of her husband, Uriah. And God spoke through Nathan to say to him, "I gave you your master's house and his wives and the kingdom of Israel and Judah. And if that had not been enough, I would have given you much, much more. Why, then, have you despised [counted worthless] the word of the LORD and done this horrible deed?" (2 Samuel 12:8-9).

Gomer, Israel, and even its kings didn't trust in the need-meeting power and provisions of God. He had actually given them everything they needed, and if it hadn't been enough he said, "I would have given you much, much more." Yet in their desire to get what they wanted when they wanted it, they betrayed their trust in God.

As I began to process Gomer's and Israel's betrayal, I was reminded how my self-centered ways are rooted in my lack of trust in God to meet all my needs. Oh, I know it in my head. I "believe" that God is my ultimate provider emotionally, relationally, physically, economically, and so on. But as soon as a need and a lot of my wants are not met immediately, what do I do? I find myself being lured by the desires of this world to meet my own needs on my own schedule. Do I really believe God is my provider? If I did I would look to him and realize the world and all its alluring trinkets will not satisfy no matter how much I have. God doesn't want me to try to meet my own needs. Instead, he wants me to put my trust in him and rely on him, the One who "satisfies every need there is" (Acts 17:25).

I found myself praying, "O God, don't let me be distracted and yield to the things of this world. I don't want to be unfaithful to you. I want to trust in you. Let me see you for who you really are—my loving all-sufficient provider."

How does Israel's unfaithfulness make God feel?
What could he have done?

It would be one thing if Gomer had left her husband for neglect or abuse. But she didn't. She had everything she needed. Yet, she prostituted herself with other men. Hosea had the right under the laws of Israel to not just divorce Gomer, but have her stoned to death. But as a *hesed* husband he showed compassion and mercy.

And how did God feel about Israel's unfaithful, adulterous behavior? "When Israel was a child," God said, "I loved him, and called my son out of Egypt. But the more I called to him, the farther he moved from me…Oh, how can I give you up Israel? How can I let you go?…My heart is torn within me, and my compassion overflows" (11:1-2; 8-9).

God could have cut them off, but he didn't. He had every right to blot them out. But the prophet Micah declared, "Where is another God like you, who pardons the sins of the survivors among his people? You cannot stay angry with your people forever, because you delight in [*hesed*] showing mercy" (Micah 7:18 NLT).

He has every right to cut me off too, but he doesn't. His *hesed* causes me to humbly thank him for his unfailing, merciful, and compassionate love toward me. I am undeserving, yet he forgives me. "Lord, allow me to never take you for granted," I prayed.

What does God do initially?

Why does he do it?

Both God and Hosea took action when they were betrayed. With a broken heart Hosea went about to frustrate his wife's plans. "I will fence her in with thornbushes. I will block her path with a wall to make her lose her way. When she runs after her lovers, she won't be able to catch them. She will search for them but not find them" (2:6-7).

And to Israel Hosea says, "You have been unfaithful to your God, hiring yourselves out like prostitutes...So now your harvests will be too small to feed you. There will be no grapes for making new wine. You may no longer stay here in the LORD's land" (9:1-3).

I was prompted to ask, Why would Hosea want to frustrate Gomer's plans? Why would God not bless Israel's harvests? Both Hosea and God appealed to the self-interest of those they loved. It is as if they were saying, "I'll keep you from fulfilling your self-serving desires until you turn to me out of pure self-preservation. Because in frustration, 'She will think, "I might as well return to my husband, for I was better off with him than I am now"'" (2:7).

---

I began to pray, "O Lord...let me suffer the consequences of my self-centered ways soon so my suffering and pain will bring me back to you."

---

God said, "They will eat and still be hungry. They will play the prostitute and gain nothing from it" (4:10). Their empty living had a purpose; their hunger would point them back in God's direction. God said, "I will return to my place until they admit their guilt and turn to me. For as soon as trouble comes, they will earnestly search for me" (5:15). His motivation for bringing punishment to Israel was to bring them back home. That's what Hosea wanted too; he wanted Gomer to come back and live with him again. What compassion...what commitment.

I was realizing that God's anger is not like mine. His anger is holy, with a holy purpose. I was reminded of what the writer of Hebrews said: "'The LORD disciplines those he loves, and he punishes each one he accepts as his child.' As you endure this divine discipline, remember that God is treating you as his own children…God's discipline is always good for us, so that we might share in his holiness" (Hebrews 12:6-7,10). I began to pray, "O Lord, allow me to quickly feel the pain of my arrogance, self-will, and stubbornness. Let me suffer the consequences of my self-centered ways soon so my suffering and pain will bring me back to you. I am empty and alone outside the boundaries of your dwelling place. Let your holy anger direct me home to you. I do not want to stray from you, O God."

What does it cost him?
What does she get?

The Lord told Hosea to "'go and love your wife again, even though she commits adultery with another lover'…So I bought her back for fifteen pieces of silver and five bushels of barley and a measure of wine" (3:1-2).

The text doesn't indicate why Hosea needed to purchase Gomer back. It is assumed she had gone into debt and became a slave. And that is what sin does, it enslaves us. The apostle Paul said, "I am sold into slavery, with sin as my master" (Romans 7:14).

The children of Israel were taught that God was so holy that he "cannot allow sin in any form" (Habakkuk 1:13). They knew a price had to be paid. They were to offer annual sacrifices of burnt offerings to God over and over again. They celebrated this reality every year during Passover. While in Egypt the death angel passed over each home that had the blood of a lamb smeared over the doorposts. A sacrifice was needed, and the Israelites continually shed the blood of bulls, goats, and lambs as a ransom—a payment for sin.

I knew, of course, that Jesus became the perfect Lamb of God to purchase all of us out of slavery to sin. "God paid a ransom," Peter stated, "to save you from the empty life you inherited from your ancestors. And the ransom he paid was not mere gold or silver. He paid for you with the precious lifeblood of Christ, the sinless, spotless Lamb of God" (1 Peter 1:18-19 NLT).

You would certainly think after such a high price God would

demand nothing short of absolute servitude from us. You would expect Hosea to say, "All right, I purchased you out of slavery, forgave you, and brought you back to live in my home again. But this time you must serve me without exception. I will not tolerate anything short of strict obedience. I will now be your master." But what do Hosea and God say?

"'I will win her back once again. I will lead her into the desert and speak tenderly to her there…She will give herself to me there, as she did long ago when she was young when I freed her from her captivity in Egypt. When that day comes,' says the LORD, 'you will call me "*my husband*" instead of "*my master*"'" (2:14-16).

Unfaithful to Hosea, Gomer deserved to remain in slavery. In their rejection of God, Israel deserves to be cut off as his chosen people. In our rebellion against God, we all deserve to be enslaved to sin and lost forever. But the God of *hesed* does more than make provision for redemption. He not only purchased us out of slavery, he restores us to a loving husband-wife relationship. Gomer got a loving relationship back. What do we get? The Almighty God who defines the meaning of relationship calls us his lover.

I began to pray, "O, Lord I cannot fathom this. I am speechless. My heart overflows. I am undeserving, yet you consider me worthy— worthy of not just life from death, but an everlasting intimate relationship with you. I have no words to express my heart of gratitude to you, O God. I am yours."

**What is "the meaning of this scripture"?**
**What does it mean to my life?**

After spending months in the book of Hosea and experiencing a deepened relationship with God, I was prepared to understand the meaning of this scripture. It had become clear that Hosea wanted Gomer back and that God wanted the children of Israel back. But why? What was God really after?

"I will make you my wife forever," God said, "showing you righteousness and justice, unfailing love and compassion. I will be faithful to you and make you mine, and you will finally know me as the LORD" (2:19-20). I began to clearly understand that all throughout

God's relationship with us, the lost and dysfunctional human race, he has shown love toward us. And it is clear he wants more than our strict obedience. He wants us to be his loving companion. And he will even inflict pain on us until we call out and say…

> "Come, let us return to the LORD. He has torn us to pieces; now he will heal us. He has injured us; now he will bandage our wounds. In just a short time he will restore us, so that we may live in his presence. Oh, that we might know the LORD! Let us press on to know him"…[now the verse Jesus quoted] "I want you to show love [*hesed*] not offer sacrifices. I want you to know me more than I want burnt offerings" (6:1-3,6).

It became clear to me that God wanted both Israel and me to know him for who he is—the Lord of *hesed*, the God who is by nature faithful, loyal, merciful, and full of compassion. And through an intimate, loving wife-husband relationship he wants me to show his kind of love toward others. When I saw that truth, I said, "I have uncovered the meaning of Hosea 6:6!"

Jesus was in effect saying to the Pharisees:

> Sure, I'm eating with tax collectors and sinners. What else would you expect me to do? I am the God of *hesed*. I have made a covenant with you to be your God forever and I am being faithful to my promise by coming as the Lamb of God to atone for your sins and restore you to a companion relationship. And you who are given to the holy Scriptures are to join me in showing *hesed* to all those who are lost and enslaved in their adulterous lives. So don't judge the tax collectors and sinners, join me in my mission of showing *hesed* to redeem and restore them back to an intimate relationship with me.

I saw it clearly. God had sent his Son as an atonement for my sin for one reason: He wanted me to be his loving companion in this life and forever. I was enslaved to sin, but he purchased me back. He now wants me to join him in showing his kind of love to others—loving God with my everything (his Great Commandment) and loving my neighbor as myself (his Great Commission). And when I drift away from his loving companionship like a dysfunctional child, in love he will cause pain in my life that is designed to direct me back to intimacy with him. And one day God will fulfill his covenant with Israel and not only bring his people back to him, but he will restore this earth to his original purpose. Then all his people, including me, will live forever in a world where there is no more pain, suffering, sin, or death, as it is prophesied in Hosea 2 and 14 and Revelation 21.

The exercise to "go learn the meaning of this Scripture" brought focus to my worldview. I read the Bible through that lens now. I see my mission in life to show *hesed* to my wife and two children as God has showed *hesed* to me. I purpose to love all those God brings into my life (my neighbors) in this way. And my motivation and passion to do this comes out of the continuing and growing desire to know God for who he is—my *hesed* companion.[1]

## YOUR PLACE WITHIN THE STORY OF SCRIPTURE

Having a deep desire for relational discovery and by asking the right questions, Dave captured both the big picture of Scripture and his story within it. There is no question that God is at work in this world today and that you are a part of his work too. The apostle Paul said that God's secret plan has been revealed, "and this is the secret plan: The Gentiles have an equal share with the Jews in all the riches inherited by God's children" (Ephesians 3:6 NLT).

---

We can more consistently experience the truths of God's Book when we see the big picture of Scripture and our place in God's story.

---

This neither lessens God's plan for Israel nor includes Gentiles in those very specific prophecies concerning Israel. But it does mean God is continuing his reconciliation of the world through his chosen people—the church. The apostle Peter wrote to the church—those redeemed Christ-followers in Asia Minor, both Jew and Gentile—and said, "You are a chosen people. You are a kingdom of priests, God's holy nation, his very own possession. This is so you can show others the goodness of God" (1 Peter 2:9 NLT). Then Peter quotes from Hosea: "'Once you were not a people; now you are the people of God. Once you received none of God's mercy; now you have received his mercy'" (1 Peter 2:10 NLT). Additionally Paul says, "God has given us the task of reconciling people to him…We are Christ's ambassadors and God is using us to speak to you" (2 Corinthians 5:18,20 NLT).

So when you read the stories of the Old Testament, do they apply to you? They do apply, yet we must see through the eyes of the Old Testament writers and through God's eyes to apply his truths to us. The truths of God's blessing, strength, assurance, protection, provision, and all the promises of an eternal home with him are yours, just as it is with the family of Abraham, Isaac, and Jacob, because of the sacrificial atonement of the Lamb of God—Jesus Christ. God has shown his *hesed* toward you too. The Old and New Testament is the revelation of himself to you. Through the power of his Book and the Holy Spirit he wants you to know him so you can enjoy all the blessings that come from his intimate companionship relationship with you. You are part of his bride—the church—and Christ is your lover.

We can more consistently experience the truths of God's book when we see the big picture of Scripture and our place in God's story. The big picture might be expressed this way:

| | |
|---|---|
| **THE CREATION:** | God created all things, including humans, for relationship. |
| *Sin:* | Humans sinned, and sin brought death (separation from God). |
| *God responds:* | God established a covenant relationship with Abraham—and through him, the children of Israel—to be their God forever. He gave a revelation of himself through the writing |

of the Hebrew Scriptures. He established a sacrificial system to cover Israel's sins until the time he would redeem and restore Israel and the whole of the human race from the slavery of sin and death.

**THE INCARNATION:** God entered the world in the form of Jesus to become the once-for-all atonement for sin. He was crucified, and raised again, and he ascended into heaven—completing that portion of his redemptive promise.

*The Holy Spirit:* Jesus returned to the Father, and the Holy Spirit was given to guarantee redemption, to form Christ's body— the church—to give an additional revelation of himself through the writings of the New Testament, and to be the living presence of Jesus within each believer.

**RE-CREATION:** God is at work in this age reconciling the world to himself through his church. Our mission with him is not complete until death is conquered and all things are restored to his original plan—that he would enjoy an eternal relationship with his people in intimate companionship. Christ will return, and we will reign with him forever. God's redemptive promise will then be complete.

The big story of creation, incarnation, and re-creation is the sweeping story from Genesis to Revelation. Yet you are included in that story, up close and personal.

| | |
|---|---|
| *Created with a special identity:* | You were created as a one-of-a-kind person to have a love relationship with God and others. |
| *Redeemed for a unique purpose:* | Pursued by God and drawn to him, you were redeemed for the purpose of bringing glory and honor to him by knowing him, being like him, and living by his ways. He completes you, and you fulfill your unique meaning in life. |
| *Fulfilling a specific destiny:* | As part of his body you have a specific destiny to fulfill: to participate in Christ's mission to reconcile the world by loving God with all your being and loving your neighbor as yourself. And then in glorious hope and expectation you will enter into your inheritance of living with God himself in a perfected relationship in a sinless and perfect world, along with those you love, for all eternity. |

Discovering your special identity, unique purpose, and specific destiny is a lifelong journey. The pages of Scripture are your roadmap, and the Holy Spirit your guide. As you probe into the living Word, God wants you to experience his *hesed*—his committed love. He wants you to equally show *hesed* to those around you. Every story of the Old Testament and passage of the New Testament hinges on this theme. As you read the Word, see yourself within God's overarching plan to reconcile the world to himself and deepen his love relationship with you as you come to know him for who he is.

Take time now to think out a heartfelt prayer to God of what this means to you. Express to him what you long for and desire in your relationship with him.

"Lord, I want to say...

_____

_____

_____

_____

_____

_____

_____

_____

_____

_____

_____

_____."

## BUT CAN YOU TRUST WHAT YOU READ?

This entire book, *Experience Your Bible,* and your relationship with the real God of the Scriptures is conditioned on one factor—that the Bible is an accurate and reliable revelation of him. If Hosea is not a historically reliable document, you have no assurance that what you have read and experienced is true or even real. That obviously means the accuracy and reliability of God's Word is a big deal.

> If we hope to enjoy the benefits of experiencing the God of the Bible, we must be sure that we have a Book that accurately represents what God inspired people to write on his behalf.

You see, before the written word, God spoke directly to Moses, Abraham, and the prophets. God also revealed himself in the flesh and spoke to us through his Son, Jesus (see Hebrews 1:1-2). These revelations of God have been recorded in written form and preserved in the pages of Scripture over thousands of years. But if the facts and events weren't carefully and truthfully recorded, then the Bible we have today is a distorted or even wholly invalid reflection of God's nature and character.

So knowing God and living in relationship with him are really dependent on our receiving and possessing an accurate revelation of him. Unless the Bible is reliable, we have no assurance that the teachings we follow and obey are true at all. Imagine, for example, that God actually gave Moses fifteen commandments, and some scribe along the way decided to eliminate five of them. We would—at best—possess an incomplete picture of what God is like and what he requires of us.

If we hope to enjoy the benefits of experiencing the God of the Bible, we must be sure that we have a Book that accurately represents what God inspired people to write on his behalf. If the Word of God was not accurately recorded and relayed to us, then we and our children will be cheated in our efforts to know the real God of the Bible.

The good news is that we can be confident in and trust God's Word. The next chapter is designed to deepen your confidence in the Bible and provide greater motivation to discover the rich treasures found within it.

# Chapter 12

# Why You Can Trust the Bible

How can you be sure the Bible you read is what God actually said? Remember that it was written thousands of years ago. How can you be sure it was copied correctly? Who is to say that large sections, even whole books, haven't been left out or distorted by people adding their own ideas? Or is there evidence that the Bible we have today is a reliable reproduction of what God inspired his writers to write? Let's explore these questions.[1]

## GOD'S WORDS HAVE BEEN RELAYED ACCURATELY

We said in the first chapter that this God-inspired book called the Bible was written over a 1500-year span through more than 40 generations by more than 40 different authors from every walk of life—shepherds, soldiers, prophets, poets, monarchs, scholars, statesmen, masters, servants, tax collectors, fishermen, and tentmakers. Its God-breathed words were put down in a variety of places: in the wilderness, in a palace, in a dungeon, on a hillside, in a prison, in exile. It was penned on the continents of Asia, Africa, and Europe and was written in three languages: Hebrew, Aramaic, and Greek. It tells hundreds of stories, records hundreds of songs, and addresses hundreds of controversial subjects. Yet with all its variety of authors, origins, and content, it achieves a miraculous continuity of theme—God's redemption of his children and the restoration of all things to his original design.

Because of the redemptive and relational purpose of the Bible, God cannot allow it to be lost, twisted, or distorted. As Jesus said, "I assure you, until heaven and earth disappear, even the smallest detail of God's law will remain until its purpose is achieved" (Matthew 5:18 NLT). He will permit nothing to impede his purpose. "Heaven and earth will disappear," Jesus said, "but my words will remain forever" (Matthew 24:35).

God is so passionate about his relationship with us that he has personally—and miraculously—provided the inspiration of his Word, supervised its transmission, and repeatedly reinforced its reliability so that all those who have open eyes and open hearts may believe it with assurance and confidence. Nations have rejected it, tyrants have tried to stamp it out, heretics have tried to distort it, societies have tried to discount and ignore it, but the evidence for the Bible's reliability is sufficient to assure us and our children that it has remained a true reflection of reality—of who God is—and that "it is stronger and more permanent than heaven and earth" (Luke 16:17 NLT).

It's not difficult to see the superintending work of God in the composition of the Old and New Testaments. Considering the process of writing and preserving manuscripts in ancient times, the fact we can be confident we have an accurate Bible is truly miraculous. None of the original manuscripts that God inspired authors to write—called *autographa*—are in existence today. What we read now are printed copies based on and translated from ancient handwritten copies of yet other copies of the original. This is because the Bible was composed and transmitted in an era before printing presses. All manuscripts had to be written by hand. Over time, the ink would fade, and the material it was written on would deteriorate. So if a document was to be preserved and passed down to the next generation, new copies would have to be made, else the document would be lost forever. Of course, these copies were made just like the originals—by hand with fading ink on deteriorating materials.

How can we be sure that the manuscripts available to us today are an accurate transmission of the originals?

But, you may rightly wonder, doesn't the making of hand-copied reproductions open up the whole transmission process to error? How do we know that a weary copier, blurry-eyed from lack of sleep, didn't skip a few critical words or leave out whole sections of Hosea or mis-quote some key verses? Or what if, during the copying of Mark's Gospel some hundred years after he wrote it, some agenda-driven, meddling scribe added five chapters of his own or twisted around the things Jesus said or did? If the words God gave to Moses, David, Matthew, or Peter were later changed or carelessly copied, how could we be sure we are coming to know the one true God? How can we be confident that the commands we obey are a true reflection of God's nature and character? What if it's true, as some critics say, that the Bible is a collection of out-dated writings that are riddled with inaccuracies and distortions? How can we be sure that the manuscripts available to us today are an accu-rate transmission of the originals?

God has not left us to wonder. He has miraculously supervised the transmission of his Word to ensure that it was relayed accurately from one generation to another.

## The Case of the Meticulous Scribes

One of the ways God ensured that his Word would be relayed accurately was by choosing, calling, and cultivating a nation of men and women who took the Book of the Law very seriously. God com-manded and instilled in the Jewish people a great reverence for his Word. From their very first days as a nation, God told them,

> Listen closely, Israel, to everything I say…Commit your-selves wholeheartedly to these commands I am giving you today. Repeat them again and again to your children. Talk about them when you are at home and when you are away on a journey, when you are lying down and when you are getting up again. Tie them to your hands as a reminder, and wear them on your forehead. Write them on the door-posts of your house and on your gates (Deuteronomy 6:3,6-9 NLT).

That attitude toward the commands of God became such a part of the Jewish identity that a class of Jewish scholars called the *Sopherim*, from a Hebrew word meaning "scribes," arose between the fifth and third centuries BC. These custodians of the Hebrew Scriptures dedicated themselves to carefully preserving the ancient manuscripts and producing new copies when necessary.

The Sopherim were eclipsed by the *Talmudic scribes*, who guarded, interpreted, and commented on the sacred texts from about AD 100 to 500. The Talmudic scribes were followed by the better-known *Masoretic scribes* (about AD 500 to 900).

The Talmudic scribes, for example, established detailed and stringent disciplines for copying a manuscript. Their rules were so rigorous that when a new copy was complete, they would give the reproduction equal authority to that of its parent because they were thoroughly convinced that they had an exact duplicate.

This was the class of people who, in the providence of God, were chosen to preserve the Old Testament text for centuries. A scribe would begin his day of transcribing by ceremonially washing his entire body. He would then garb himself in full Jewish dress before sitting at his desk. As he wrote, if he came to the Hebrew name of God, he could not begin writing the name with a quill newly dipped in ink for fear it would smear the page. Once he began writing the name of God, he could not stop or allow himself to be distracted. Even if a king was to enter the room, the scribe was obligated to continue without interruption until he finished penning the holy name of the one true God.

The Talmudic guidelines for copying manuscripts also required the following:

- The scroll must be made of the skin of a ceremonially clean animal.
- Each skin must contain a specified number of columns, equal throughout the entire book.
- The length of each column must extend no less than 48 lines or more than 60 lines.

- The column breadth must consist of exactly 30 letters.
- The space of a thread must appear between every consonant.
- The breadth of nine consonants had to be inserted between each section.
- A space of three lines had to appear between each book.
- The fifth book of Moses (Deuteronomy) had to conclude exactly with a full line.
- Nothing—not even the shortest word—could be copied from memory; everything had to be copied letter by letter.
- The scribe must count the number of times each letter of the alphabet occurred in each book and compare it to the original.[2]

God instilled in these scribes such a painstaking reverence for the Hebrew Scriptures to ensure the amazingly accurate transmission of the Book of the Law so you and I—and our children—would have an accurate revelation of God.

Until recently, however, we had no way of knowing just how amazing the preservation of the Old Testament had been. Before 1947, the oldest complete Hebrew manuscript dated to AD 900. But with the discovery of 223 manuscripts and many more partial manuscripts and fragments in caves on the west side of the Dead Sea, we now have Old Testament manuscripts that have been dated by paleographers to around 125 BC. These Dead Sea Scrolls, as they are called, are a thousand years older than any previously known manuscripts.[3]

But here's the exciting part: Once the Dead Sea Scrolls were translated and compared with modern versions, the modern Hebrew Bible proved to be identical, word for word, in more than 95 percent of the text. (The 5 percent variation consisted mainly of spelling variations. For example, of the 166 words in Isaiah 53, only 17 letters were in question. Of those, 10 letters were a matter of spelling, and 4 were stylistic changes; the remaining 3 letters comprised the word *light,* which was added in verse 11.)[4]

In other words, the greatest manuscript discovery of all time revealed that a thousand years of copying the Old Testament had produced only excruciatingly minor variations, none of which altered the clear meaning of the text or brought the manuscript's fundamental integrity into question.

Critics will still make their pronouncements in contradiction to the evidence. However, the overwhelming weight of evidence affirms that God has preserved his Word and accurately relayed it through the centuries—so that when you pick up an Old Testament today, you can be utterly confident that you are holding a well-preserved, fully reliable document.

## The Case of the New Testament Text

As you know, the Hebrew scribes did not copy the manuscripts of the New Testament. There were several reasons. The official Jewish leadership did not endorse Christianity; the letters and histories circulated by the New Testament writers were not then thought of as official Scripture; and these documents were not written in the Hebrew language, but rather in forms of Greek and Aramaic. Thus, the same formal disciplines were not followed in the transmission of these writings from one generation to another. In the case of the New Testament, God did a new thing to ensure that the blessing of his Word would be accurately preserved for us and our children.

Historians evaluate the textual reliability of ancient literature according to two standards: 1) the time interval between the original and the earliest copy; and 2) how many manuscript copies are available.

For example, virtually everything we know today about Julius Caesar's exploits in the Gallic Wars (58 to 51 BC) is derived from ten manuscript copies of Caesar's work *The Gallic Wars*. The earliest of these copies dates to a little less than a thousand years from the time the original was written. Our modern text of Livy's *History of Rome* relies on 1 partial manuscript and 19 much later copies that are dated from 400 to 1000 years *after* the original writing (see chart below).[5]

| TEXTUAL RELIABILITY STANDARDS APPLIED TO CLASSICAL LITERATURE | | | | | |
|---|---|---|---|---|---|
| Author | Book | Date written | Earliest copies | Time gap | Number of copies |
| Homer | *Iliad* | 800 BC | c. 400 BC | c. 400 years | 643 |
| Herodotus | *History* | 480–425 BC | c. AD 900 | c. 1350 years | 8 |
| Thucydides | *History* | 460–400 BC | c. AD 900 | c. 1300 years | 8 |
| Plato | | 400 BC | c. AD 900 | c. 1300 years | 7 |
| Demosthenes | | 300 BC | c. AD 1100 | c. 1400 years | 200 |
| Caesar | *Gallic Wars* | 100–44 BC | c. AD 900 | c. 1000 years | 10 |
| Livy | *History of Rome* | 59 BC–AD 17 | fourth century | c. 400 years | 1 partial |
| | | | tenth century | c. 1000 years | 19 |
| Tacitus | *Annals* | AD 100 | c. AD 1100 | c. 1000 years | 20 |
| Pliny Secundus | *Natural History* | AD 61–113 | c. AD 850 | c. 750 years | 7 |

By comparison, the text of Homer's *Iliad* is much more reliable. It is supported by 643 manuscript copies in existence today, with a mere 400-year time gap between the date of composition and the earliest of these copies.

The textual evidence for Livy and Homer is considered more than adequate for historians to use in validating the original, but this evidence pales in comparison to what God performed in the case of the New Testament text.

The New Testament Has No Equal

Using this accepted standard for evaluating the textual reliability of ancient writings, the New Testament stands alone. It has no equal. No other book of the ancient world can even approach its reliability. (See chart of "Textual Reliability Standards Applied to the Bible.")[6]

Nearly *25,000* manuscripts or fragments of manuscripts of the New Testament repose in the libraries and universities of the world.

The earliest of these discovered so far is a fragment of John's Gospel located in the John Rylands Library of the University of Manchester, England; it has been dated to within *50 years* of when the apostle John penned the original![7]

| TEXTUAL RELIABILITY STANDARDS APPLIED TO THE BIBLE | | | | |
|---|---|---|---|---|
| Author | Book | Earliest copies | Time gap | Number of copies |
| John | New Testament | c. AD 130 | 50-plus years | Fragments |
| The rest of the New Testament books | | c. AD 200 (books) | 100 years | |
| | | c. AD 250 (most of New Testament) | 150 years | |
| | | c. AD 325 (complete New Testament) | 225 years | 5600-plus Greek manuscripts |
| | | c. AD 366–384 (Latin Vulgate translation) | 284 years | |
| | | c. AD 400–500 (other translations) | 400 years | 19,000-plus translated manuscripts |
| | | **TOTALS** | 50–400 years | 24,900-plus manuscripts |

Since the time the original manuscripts were written—more than 1900 years ago—many attempts have been made to refute or destroy the Bible. However, God's Word has not only prevailed, it has also proliferated. Voltaire, the noted eighteenth-century French writer and skeptic, predicted that within a hundred years of his time Christianity would be but a footnote in history. Ironically, in 1828, 50 years after his death, the Geneva Bible Society moved into his house and began to use his printing press to produce thousands of Bibles to distribute worldwide. "People are like grass that dies away," Peter wrote, quoting

Isaiah the prophet, "but the word of the Lord will last forever" (1 Peter 1:24-25 NLT).

No other book in history has been so widely distributed in so many languages. Distribution of the Bible reaches into the billions of copies! According to the United Bible Society's 2008 report, in that year alone, member organizations distributed 28.4 million complete Bibles and just under 300 million selections from the Bible.[8] They also report that the Bible or portions of the Bible have been translated into more than 2400 languages. And amazingly, these languages represent the primary vehicles of communication for well over 90 percent of the world's population![9]

## GOD'S WORD HAS BEEN RECORDED EXACTLY

We can be confident that the text of both the Old and New Testaments has been handed down over the centuries with precision and accuracy. In other words, we can be assured that what was written down initially is what we have today. But a more basic question arises. Were the words from God recorded exactly as he intended? When these inspired writers were recording historical events, were they chronologically close to those events so that we can have confidence in the accuracy of what they wrote?

---

God could have spoken through anyone, from anywhere, to write his words about Christ. But to give us additional confidence in the truth, he worked through eyewitnesses.

---

Many ancient writings adhere only loosely to the facts of the events they report. Some highly regarded authors of the ancient world, for example, report events that took place many years before they were born and in countries they had never visited. While their accounts may be largely factual, historians admit that greater credibility must be granted to writers who are both geographically and chronologically close to the events they report.

With that in mind, look at the loving care God took when he

inspired the writing of the New Testament. The overwhelming weight of scholarship confirms that the accounts of Jesus' life, the history of the early church, and the letters that form the bulk of the New Testament were all written by men who were either eyewitnesses to the events they recorded or contemporaries of eyewitnesses. God selected Matthew, Mark, and John to write three of the four Gospels. These were men who could say such things as, "This report is from an eyewitness giving an accurate account" (John 19:35). He spoke through Luke the physician to record the third Gospel and the book of Acts. Luke, a meticulous and careful writer, used as "source material the reports circulating among us from the early disciples and other eyewitnesses of what God [did] in fulfillment of his promises" (Luke 1:2 NLT).

God could have spoken through anyone, from anywhere, to write his words about Christ. But to give us additional confidence in the truth, he worked through eyewitnesses such as John, who said, "We are telling you about what we ourselves have actually seen and heard" (1 John 1:3 NLT). He worked through Peter, who declared, "We did not follow cunningly devised fables when we made known to you the power and coming of our Lord Jesus Christ, but were eyewitnesses of His majesty" (2 Peter 1:16 NKJV). And whom did he choose as his most prolific writer? The apostle Paul, whose dramatic conversion from persecutor of Christians to planter of churches made him perhaps the most credible witness of all!

But God didn't stop there. Those through whom he transmitted his inspired Word were also apostles. These men could rely on their own eyewitness experiences, and they could appeal to the firsthand knowledge of their contemporaries, even their most rabid opponents (see Acts 2:32; 3:15; 13:31; 1 Corinthians 15:3-8). They not only said, "Look, we saw this," or "We heard that," but they were also so confident in what they wrote as to say, in effect, "Check it out," "Ask around," and "You know it as well as I do!" Such challenges demonstrate a supreme confidence that the "God-breathed" Word was recorded exactly as God spoke it (2 Timothy 3:16 NIV).

Such careful inspiration and supervision of the Bible underlines God's purpose—that not a single piece of this revelation about himself or the human condition be left to chance or recorded incorrectly. Ample evidence exists to suggest that he was very selective in the people he chose to record his words—they were people who for the most part had firsthand knowledge of key events and who were credible channels to record and convey exactly those truths he wanted us to know.*

## GOD'S WORD HAS BEEN REINFORCED EXTERNALLY

God did not stop working after he had brought about the development of the massive textual evidence for the reliability of his Word. He has since worked to reinforce the evidence through external means.

A routine criterion in examining the reliability of an historical document is whether *other* historical material confirms or denies the internal testimony of the document itself. Historians ask, "What sources, apart from the literature under examination, substantiate its accuracy and reliability?"

In the case of the New Testament, for example, it is so extensively quoted in the ancient manuscripts of nonbiblical authors that all 27 books, from Matthew through Revelation, could be reconstructed virtually word for word, except for 11 verses.

The writings of early Christians like Eusebius (AD 339) in his *Ecclesiastical History* (III.39) and Irenaeus (AD 180) in his *Against Heresies* (Book III) reinforce the text of the apostle John's writings. Clement of Rome (AD 95), Ignatius (AD 70–110), Polycarp (AD 70–156), and Titian (AD 170) offer external confirmation of other New Testament accounts. Non-Christian historians such as the first-century Roman historian Tacitus (AD 55–117) and the Jewish historian Josephus (AD 37–100) confirm the substance of many scriptural accounts. These and other outside sources substantiate the accuracy of the biblical record like that of no other book in history.[10]†

These extrabiblical references, however, are not the only external

---

\* A comprehensive treatment of the internal evidence test is covered in chapters 3, 4, and 21 of Josh McDowell, *The New Evidence That Demands a Verdict*, rev. ed.(Nashville, TN: Thomas Nelson, 1999).

† For more information on the confirmation of the Bible's reliability in extrabiblical sources, see chapters 3 and 4 of *The New Evidence That Demands a Verdict*.

evidences that support the Bible's reliability. The very stones cry out that God's Word is true. Over and over again through the centuries, the reliability of the Bible has been regularly and consistently supported by archaeology. Consider the following evidences recently published in *The Apologetics Study Bible for Students*, of which I (Sean) was the general editor.

### Biblical Archaeology

Until the late eighteenth century, the pursuit of biblical artifacts in the Near East was the work of amateur treasure hunters whose methods included grave-robbing. The discovery of the Rosetta Stone in Egypt by Napoleon's army in 1799 changed everything. Biblical archaeology gradually became the domain of respected archaeologists. The discovery of ancient ruins all across the Near East has shed new light on peoples and events mentioned in Scripture. We can now better understand the customs and lifestyles that are foreign to the modern mind.

Archaeology has also established the historicity of the people and events described in the Bible, yielding over 25,000 finds that relate either directly or indirectly to Scripture. Moreover, the historical existence of some 30 individuals named in the New Testament, and nearly 60 in the Old Testament, has been confirmed through archaeological and historical research. Only a small fraction of possible biblical sites have been excavated in the Holy Land, and even regarding existing excavations, much more could be published. Nonetheless, the archaeological data we now possess, such as the examples that follow, clearly indicates that the Bible is historically reliable and is not the product of myth, superstition, or embellishment (John 3:12; 2 Peter 1:16; 1 John 1:1-2).

**Ancient Corinth.** Archaeological research conducted in Corinth from 1928 to 1947 startled researchers with two objects relating to Paul's epistles to the Corinthian and Roman churches. A Latin inscription dating to about AD 50 carved into an ancient sidewalk identifies Paul's co-laborer "Erastus" as the city treasurer (Romans 16:23). The inscription says Erastus laid a portion of sidewalk at his own expense in appreciation for being elected as treasurer. Moreover, a stone platform used to hold public lectures, official business, and trials, and to render judgments, was unearthed in 1935. It was identified as the *bema* seat. *Bema* is the same Greek word Paul used to describe the "judgment" seat of Christ (2 Corinthians 5:10) at which all Christians must appear for their rewards (1 Corinthians 3:10-17).

**The Arch of Titus.** When Jesus talked with his disciples on the Mount of Olives about the buildings of the temple, he said, "Do you see all these things? Truly I tell you, not one stone here will be left on another; every one will be thrown down!" (Matthew 24:2). The accuracy of Jesus' prophecy is demonstrated by the Arch of Titus, which was constructed as a victory memorial for Emperor Titus (AD 79–81) by his younger brother Emperor Domitian (AD 81–96). Located in Rome between the ancient Forum and the Coliseum, the marble arch depicts the transportation of spoils (the menorah and sacred trumpets) from the ransacked Jerusalem temple.

In addition to this important evidence, excavations in the area of the lower street along the southwest corner of the Jerusalem Temple Mount in the 1970s revealed large stones that had been toppled from the heights by the Romans in their military campaign of AD 70. Today, none of the original building structures remain standing on the temple mount. The depictions and inscription on the Arch of Titus, as well as the rubble found at the Temple Mount in Jerusalem, provide historical verification for the fulfillment of Jesus' prediction that the Jewish temple would be utterly destroyed.

**The Babylonian Chronicles** are a series of tablets with cuneiform writing that describes important events transpiring between the eighth and third centuries BC. One particular chronicle covers the period between 605–594 BC, recording the military exploits of Babylonian King Nebuchadnezzar II (605–562 BC) and his invasion of Jerusalem (2 Kings 23). It recounts how in 605 BC Nebuchadnezzar was crowned king after the death of his father, Nabopolassar. The Chronicles say that by 599 BC Nebuchadnezzar's army advanced to Syria, continued westward to Judah, and arrived there in March 597 BC. Once there the king invaded Jerusalem, took captive King Jehoiakim (609–597 BC), and crowned his replacement King Zedekiah (597–586 BC; 2 Kings 24:10-20).

Robert Koldewey discovered more supporting evidence for these events in Babylonian ration records (595 BC), which document the food rations given to Jehoiakim and his royal family while in captivity (2 Kings 24:8-16). Additionally, hastily inscribed shards known as the Lachish Letters record Israelites' desperate pleas in the hours immediately before Babylonian forces overwhelmed Israel's military outposts some 25 miles outside Jerusalem. These strong archaeological evidences support the biblical record describing Jerusalem's final days under siege by Nebuchadnezzar.

> In addition to Balaam, nearly 60 other Old Testament figures have been either historically or archaeologically identified.

**The Balaam inscription.** The story of Balaam and his talking donkey (Numbers 22:22-40) was derided by critical scholars for many decades. Even the existence of Balaam was doubted. This view began to change in 1967, when archaeologists collected a crumbled plaster Aramaic text in the rubble of an ancient building in Deir 'Alla (Jordan). The text contains 50 lines written in faded red and black ink. The inscription reads, "Warnings from the Book of Balaam the son of Beor. He was a seer of the gods" (Numbers 22:5; Joshua 24:9). Though the building in which the text was found dates back to only the eighth century BC (during the reign of King Uzziah; see Isaiah 6:1), the condition of the plaster and ink of the text itself indicates that it is most likely much older, dating to the time of the biblical Balaam.

In addition to Balaam, nearly 60 other Old Testament figures have been either historically or archaeologically identified. These include kings David (1 Samuel 16:13), Jehu (2 Kings 9:2), Omri (1 Kings 16:22), Uzziah (Isaiah 6:1), Jotham (2 Kings 15:7), Hezekiah (Isaiah

37:1), Jehoiachin (2 Chronicles 36:8), Shalmaneser V (2 Kings 17:3), Tiglath-Pileser III (1 Chronicles 5:6), Sargon II (Isaiah 20:1), Sennacherib (Isaiah 36:1), Nebuchadnezzar (Daniel 2:1), Belshazzar (Daniel 5:1), Cyrus (Isaiah 45:1), and others.

**The Ebla Tablets.** Discovered by Italian archaeologist Paolo Matthiae in 1976 at Tell Mardikh in Aleppo (Syria), the Ebla Tablets represent a royal archive of over 16,000 clay tablets. Dating from 2400 BC, the records give us a glimpse into the lifestyle, vocabulary, commerce, geography, and religion of the peoples who lived near Canaan (later called Israel) in the time immediately before Abraham, Isaac, and Jacob. Translations of several tablets by Giovanni Pettinato in his *Archives of Ebla: An Empire Inscribed in Clay* support the existence of biblical cities such as Sodom (Genesis 19:1), Zeboiim (Genesis 14:2,8), Admah (Genesis 10:19), Hazor (1 Kings 9:15), Megiddo (1 Chronicles 7:29), Canaan (Genesis 48:4), and Jerusalem (Jeremiah 1:15).

Further, the tablets include personal names like those of biblical persons, such as Nahor (Genesis 11:22-25), Israel (Genesis 32:28), Eber (Genesis 10:21-25), Michael (Numbers 13:13), and Ishmael (Genesis 16:11). Regarding vocabulary, the tablets contain certain words similar to those used in the Bible, such as *tehom*, which in Genesis 1:2 is translated as "the deep." In addition to these correspondences, the tablets provide information related to Hebrew literary style and religion, helping us to understand the civilizations in the region that became known as Israel.[11]

Repeatedly throughout the previous two centuries, the astounding accuracy of God's Word has been confirmed externally. This is a very different case from that of the Book of Mormon, for example, for which there is no external support, despite much research and exploration. The external evidence for the Bible is an extremely rare phenomenon, and it makes the Bible unique compared to other religious writings of the world.

The evidence for the reliability of the Old and New Testaments is not only convincing and compelling, it is also a clear and praiseworthy indication of how God lovingly supervised its transmission. He wants you to be confident that when you discover him and his ways within the pages of his Word you are discovering the real "God who is passionate about his relationship with you" (Exodus 34:14 NLT).

# A Final Word

e (Josh and Sean) hope you have gleaned some insights through these chapters that will help you better explore the depths of God's Word. We have come a long way in such a short time. To summarize:

We have examined how the Bible has a doctrinal purpose. It gives us rational truths that we can understand with the mind. It instructs us on what we should believe about God, ourselves, and all of life. It enables us to see life as God sees it and that is the very basis of our biblical worldview.

We also explored how the Bible has a behavioral purpose. We saw how God's laws and instructions act as boundaries to tell us what is right and wrong. We discovered how living out God's ways is in our best interest. God gave us his Word so we could live out his truth correctly. And as we do we live happy, fulfilled lives that honor him.

But we discussed how we can miss the central purpose of God's Word unless we understand that all of it has been given to us within a relational context. God gave us the Bible because he wants an intimate loving relationship with us and wants us to enjoy intimate loving relationships with one another. And because he is a relational God who made us in his relational image, he wants us to experience him through his Word. He wants us to experience his Word with others. Our hope of this book is that it will encourage you to go beyond mere study and experience your Bible.

Our hope too is that your journey through these pages will go beyond you benefiting personally. We hope you will share it with others. So we encourage you to get together with your Christian friends and make studying the Bible a consistent experience. So many small groups today center around fellowship and the sharing of people's lives with each other. And that is important. But what is needed is the additional fellowshipping around God's Word. When you make God's Word the central focus of your time together you can truly experience God and experience his Word with one another. That is when the Body of Christ grows together and his truth begins to be demonstrated to the world around us as truly relevant to life.

Our prayer for you is that you will never again see doctrine or God's commands as simply truths to believe and apply to life. For as important as they are, and they are critically important, God's truths are a means to deepen our relationship with him. Perhaps a fitting close to our journey together is a quotation from King David's prayer. David was a man after God's own heart. And he saw all of God's commands within the context of his relationship with his loving Lord.

> *Teach me your decrees, O LORD;*
> *    I will keep them to the end.*
> *Give me understanding and I will obey your instructions;*
> *    I will put them into practice with all my heart.*
> *Make me walk along the path of your commands,*
> *    for that is where my happiness is found.*
> *Give me an eagerness for your laws*
> *    rather than a love for money!*
> *Turn my eyes from worthless things,*
> *    and give me life through your word.*
> *Reassure me of your promise,*
> *    made to those who fear you.*
> *Help me abandon my shameful ways;*
> *    for your regulations are good.*
> *I long to obey your commandments!*
> *    Renew my life with your goodness.*
> Psalm 119:33-40

# ADDITIONAL
# RESOURCES

# NOTES

# Additional Resources

You will not uncover all the riches of the Scriptures in just a week, month, or year. It takes time and effort. The added resources within the upcoming pages perhaps may help you in that process. These resources include:

- *Title Chart of Ephesians*
  These are the insights gleaned by Sean's high-school students as a result of their study of Ephesians.

- *The Paraphrase*
  Guidelines in creating your own paraphrase of Scripture passages.

- *The Topical Study*
  Guidelines on developing Bible studies on a particular topic.

- *The Biographical Study*
  Guidelines on developing a study of a person in Scripture.

- *Reference Chart for a Crisis Bible Study*
  A categorized list of scriptural references to find passages that apply in times of need or hurt.

| SAMPLE TITLE CHART BY HIGH SCHOOL STUDENTS | | | | | | |
|---|---|---|---|---|---|---|
| Ephesians: By God's Grace and Truth, Live Like Christ in Unity | | | | | | |
| Chapters | 1 | 2 | 3 | 4 | 5 | 6 |
| Chapter Titles | Salvation Through Christ | Grace Alone | Salva-tion for Gentiles | Christ-Like Living | Wise Living | Stand Firm |
| Paragraph Titles | :1-2 Greeting<br><br>:3-14 Blessings<br><br>:15-23 God's Great-ness and Power | :1-10 Saved by Grace<br><br>:11-22 Unity | :1-13 Mystery of Christ<br><br>:14-21 God's Power | :1-16 One Body in Christ<br><br>:17-Ch. 5:5 Be Imitators of God | :6-21 Be Wise<br><br>:22-23 Hus-bands and Wives | :1-4 Chil-dren and Parents<br><br>:5-9 Slaves and Masters<br><br>:10-20 Armor of God<br><br>:21-24 Clos-ing State-ments |
| Key Verse: | 9 | 5 | 6 | 15,16 | 18 | 11 |
| Key Word: | Promise | Made alive | Fellow heirs | Whole body | Walk | Armor |

Observations:

- Good works are the result of salvation, not the cause.
- Part of the reason we were created is to do good works.
- Salvation is a gift from God, not from our efforts.

# The Paraphrase

Another helpful step in understanding and teaching the Scriptures is doing a paraphrase to see the details of the passage you are studying.

## How to See the Details of a Passage by Writing a Paraphrase

A. Definition: To paraphrase a passage of Scripture is to study a passage and to restate it in your own words.

B. How a paraphrase can help you:

1. To paraphrase a passage requires that you think through each thought and word of the passage sufficiently enough to restate it. It will clarify your thinking of the truths presented.

2. It also can help your communication of those spiritual truths to others. You should seek to express the truths in terms that would be understood easily by someone else today. Put it into contemporary English. (Eugene Peterson's *The Message* is one modern paraphrase that would be good to study as an example.)

C. How to use variety in paraphrase.

1. *A normal paraphrase:* One type of paraphrase takes the passage one phrase at a time and rephrases it in your own words. It is important not to change just a few words in the passage but to change the entire phrase and leave almost no word the same.

2. *A condensed paraphrase:* You might try to boil a passage down to two-thirds, one-half, or even one-third its original length. Try not to omit the essential parts. This type of paraphrase is especially good for long passages or narrative passages.

3. *An expanded paraphrase:* You might expand the passage to even as much as twice its original length. You are seeking to fully explain its meaning. This type of paraphrase includes interpretations and explanations of things that are not clear. It is very appropriate for doctrinal passages rather than narrative.

4. *An imaginative paraphrase:* Use your imagination in paraphrasing.

   a. Sometimes try changing illustrations into modern illustrations. Instead of saying the Word of God is "sharper than any two-edged sword," you might say it is "sharper than any surgeon's scalpel."

   b. You might imagine that you are writing to some particular person today. For example, you want to paraphrase one of Paul's epistles. So, you imagine that you are writing a friend who is a new Christian, and you try to explain the truths found in the epistle in the language that you would normally use if you were writing him a letter or an e-mail.

# The Topical Study

I. **What is a topical study?**

   A. Instead of studying a book or a portion of a book, in a topical study you are seeking to determine what is taught by Scripture on a particular subject. For example, you may wish to study what the Bible has to say about the subject "laziness."

   B. For a doctrinal study, you simply choose a doctrinal topic, such as the doctrine of justification.

   C. Because of time available, you may choose to limit your subject by limiting the portion of Scripture from which you obtain your material. For example: "The doctrine of Christ in Colossians," or "The use of the term *children* in the writings of John."

   D. The key to a good topical study is the selection of a good topic.

II. **How to locate material for a topical study**

   A. *Use a concordance.* Look up the use of words that relate to your topic.

   B. *Cross-references.* Once you have found some passages that relate to your topic, you can often find cross-references from these to other passages.

   C. *Bible dictionary.* This may give you both good

information and further scriptural references concerning your topic.

D. *Subject listings.* Sometimes reference Bibles list Scripture references according to subject. There are also topical Bibles, such as Nave's Topical Bible, which write out the entire text or various passages that relate to certain topics.

E. *Limited study.* If you have limited your subject to a certain portion of Scripture, such as "Paul's prayers in his epistles," you might have to read or scan the material to locate the sections you want.

## III. How to arrange what you locate

A. Once you have located your material, study it and make any notes concerning things you want to remember.

B. Study your notes and categorize them. Group together similar ideas under similar topics. The different emphasis of the various verses will suggest various topics for the outline. As you begin to categorize verses, this may suggest to your mind further study in certain areas of the topic.

C. Next, work your material into a logical outline. Begin with a rough tentative outline and polish it as you progress. Try to fit all of your material into the outline.

# The Biographical Study

This is actually a specialized topical study—the topic here being a person.

I. **How to research a biographical study**

   A. *Things to keep in mind.*

   1. Find your material in a similar manner as you would for a topical study.

   2. Be careful if you use a Bible dictionary that you do not let it do your thinking for you or predispose your mind to certain conclusions. It may be best to read the Bible dictionary article after you have done your own thinking.

   3. Some Bible characters have more than one name, such as Saul for Paul, Cephas and Simon for Peter, Israel for Jacob. Be sure you have all the references for the person.

   4. Sometimes biblical names are used for more than one person—for example, Saul, John, Mary, and so on. Be sure that you are reading about the person you want to study.

   5. Some characters have such a large portion of Scripture devoted to them that you may want to limit your study to a particular phase or aspect of

that person's life. (Example: "The prayer life of the apostle Paul.")

B. *Things to look for.* The following suggests certain items to look for in doing a research. Sometimes, because of lack of information on an individual, it will not be possible to find all of them. This does not pretend to be an exhaustive list but simply a guide. You will think of other areas for study as you find information on the person being studied. For instance, if you were doing a biographical study of David, you could ask the following questions (which of course could be used for any Bible character):

1. Background.

   a. What were the circumstances surrounding his birth—when, where, and so on?

   b. Who were his parents and family? What were they like? What was their spiritual condition?

   c. How did environment and early training influence his later life?

   d. What other factors prepared him for later life?

2. Major factors of adult life.

   a. What were his major occupation and achievements in life?

   b. What was he noted for?

   c. What people were important in his life? His friends, his enemies, his family? What influence did others have on him and vice versa?

   d. Geography—where did he live and work?

   e. What was his relationship to God? How did this affect his life and accomplishments?

   f. Did he write any portion of Scripture? What does it show about him?

3. Major events.

    a. What were the major events of his life? What were the major crises?

    b. What were the various periods or phases of his life? What were the pivotal points that divide these periods?

    c. What were the manner, cause, and effect of his death?

4. Character.

    a. What sort of character did he have?

    b. What were his strong points?

    c. What were his weak points?

    d. What were the causes and results of the strong and weak points of his character?

    e. What were his specific faults and sins? What were the consequences of this?

    f. What were his specific strengths and gifts? What resulted from his use of them?

    g. What was his general attitude toward life and toward others?

    h. What was his spiritual status?

    i. What basic principles seemed to guide his life and his work?

5. Influence.

    a. What effect did he have on his contemporaries?

    b. What influence did he have on subsequent history?

    c. Concerning an Old Testament character, find out the following:

        1. Could he be considered a type of Christ? If so, in what way?

2. How does the New Testament represent
   him, if it does?

6. Details. Do not overlook details. They add color
   and often prove to be very significant.

## II. How to organize your material in a biographical study

A. You may want to arrange your material in outline
   form. Some of the above suggestions (subpoint B
   under point I) of what to look for may suggest other
   categories.

B. You may want to write a character sketch of the person.

C. Conclude your story by writing a section on suggested
   personal applications to your own life. These could
   be derived from the positive or negative aspects of the
   person's life you study, or both.

# Reference Chart for a Crisis Bible Study

**Affection Needs**

Acts 27

**Alcohol and Drugs**

Gen. 1:28; Num. 6:2-4; Deut. 6:4;
Ps. 55:22; 104; Prov. 20:1; 23:20;
23:29-35; 31:4-6; Isa. 5:11; Matt. 11:19;
16:27-29; 27:34; Mark 15:23; Luke
7:33,34; 10:34; John 2:9,10; 14:6;
Rom. 12:1; 13:1-5, 13; 14:21; 1
Cor. 5:11; 6:10-12; 6:19,20; Gal. 5:16-21;
Eph. 5:18; Col. 3:2; 1 Tim. 2:5; 5:23; 1
Thess. 5:4-8; 1 Pet. 1:13; 2:13-17; 4:3,4;
5:7; Rev. 9:20,21; 18:23; 21:8; 22:15

**Anger**

Ps. 2:5-9; 7:11; 10; 95:11; 130:3,4;
Isa. 48:9; Dan. 9:9; Amos 5:18-20;
Nah. 1:2,3; 1:6-8; Mark 3:5; Rom. 1:18;
2:5; 1 Thess. 1:10; 2:1b; Prov. 22:24,25;
24:29; 26:24

*Warning Against Human Anger*

Ps. 37:8; Prov. 10:18; 14:27,29; 15:1,18;
16:32; 20:3,22; 27:5,6; 29:11,20,22;
Eccl. 7:9; Matt. 5:22; 7:1-5; Luke
17:3,4; Rom. 12:19; 14:4; 2 Cor. 7:8-10;
Gal. 5:20; Eph. 4:26-32; Col. 3:8; 2
Tim. 4:2; Heb. 12:15; James 1:19,20;
3:3-14; 4:1; 5:9

*Dealing with It*

Gen. 4:5-7; Prov. 15:28; 19:19; 22:24,25;
25:15; Matt. 2:16; Mark 10:14; John 4

*Effects*

Ps. 73; Prov. 14:17; 25:28; Matt. 5:38,44;
Eph. 4:30,31

**Anxiety**

*Bad*

Ps. 55:22; 121; Matt. 6:25-34; Acts 27;
Phil. 4:6,7; 1 Pet. 5:7

*Good*

2 Cor. 11:28; Phil. 2:20

*"Cures"—Dealing with It*

John 14:1-3; 14:18,27; Phil. 4:4-9;
Heb. 13:6; James 1:22; 1 John 4:18

**Compassion**

Matt. 9:36; 14:14; 15:32; 20:34; Mark
1:41; 6:34; 8:2; 10:21; Luke 19:41-44

**Death**

Ps. 23:6; Prov. 3:21-16; 14:32; 1 Cor.
15:54-58; Phil. 1:21,23; Heb. 2:14,15

**Decision Making**

2 Tim. 3:15-18; Heb. 11:23-27

## Depression [Despair]

Gen. 4:6,7; Ex. 6:9; Num. 11:10-15; 1 Kings 19; Job 3; Ps. 23:4; 27; 32; 34:15-17; 38; 40:1-3; 51; 69; 88; 102; 103:13,14; 121; Prov. 18:14; Lamentations; Matt. 5:12; 11:28-30; 26:37,38; 26:75; John 4:1-3; 15:10,11; Acts 27; Rom. 8:28; 15:13; 2 Cor. 4:8,9; Eph. 1:3-14

### Dealing with It

John 14:1-14; 14:26,27; Col. 1:16,17; Heb. 1:3; 13:5

### Preventing It

Phil. 4:11-13; 4:8

## Desire

Gen. 3:6; Ex. 20:17; Prov. 10:3,24; 11:6; 28:25; Matt. 6:21; Luke 12:31-34; Rom. 13:14; Gal. 5:16; Eph. 2:3; Titus 2:12; 3:3; Jas. 1:13-16; 1 John 2:16; Jude 18; 1 Pet. 1:14; 4:2,3

## Discipline

Prov. 3:11,12; 13:24; 19:18; 22:6,15; 23:13; 29:15; 1 Cor. 5:1-13; 11:29-34; 2 Cor. 2:1-11; 12:7-10; Eph. 6:1-4; 1 Tim. 4:7; Heb. 12:5-11

## Divorce

Gen. 2:18-25; Ex. 20:14; Deut. 24:1-4; Isa. 50:1; Jer. 3:1; Mal. 2:16; Matt. 5:2; 5:27,28; 5:31,32; 6:14,15; 19:3-9; Mark 10:2-12; Rom. 6:1-2; 12:1-2; 13:14; 1 Cor. 7:10-24; 7:33-34; 7:39-40; Jas. 5:16

### Causes Of

1 Cor. 7:10-15

### Preventing

1 Sam. 12:33

## Endurance

Ps. 40:1-3; John 11; Acts 27; 2 Cor. 12:7-10; Heb. 12:5-11

## Envy

Titus 3:5; Jas. 3:14-16; 1 Pet. 2:1

## Fear

Gen. 3:10; Ps. 103; 121; Prov. 10:24; 29:25; Matt. 10:26-31; Acts 27; 2 Tim. 1:7; Heb. 2:14,15; 1 Pet. 3:6; 3:13,14; 1 John 4:18

## Financial

Deut. 8:11-14; Job 31:24-25; 31:28; Ps. 49:10-12; 52:5-7; 62:10; Prov. 3:9; 10:9; 11:1; 15:27; 17:23; 19:17; 22:7; 23:4,5; 27:24; 28:20; 30:7-10; Eccl. 5:10; Matt. 6:24-34; 18:23-25; 19:16-24; 25:14-30; Mark 6:7-11; 8:36; Luke 12:13-21; 16:19f; Rom. 13:6-8; 1 Cor. 16:2; 2 Cor. 8:14,15; 9:7; Phil. 4:18,19; 1 Tim. 6:7,10; Heb: 13:5

### Causes Of

Ex. 20:17; Ps. 72:2,3; Prov. 3:9-10; 3:27-28; 11:15; 11:24,25; 14:21; 17:18; 19:15,17; 21:5; 22:7; 22:26,27; 28:20,22; Eccl. 5:15-17; Mal. 8:10; Luke 3:11; 6:38; 12:15-21; Rom. 18:8,9; Gal. 6:10; 1 Thess. 3:10; Rev. 3:17

### Dealing with

Gen. 1:28; Ex. 20:15,27; Ps. 50:10-12; 50:15; Ps. 55:22; Matt. 6:25-34; 25:14-29; 1 Pet. 5:7

## Forgiveness

Ps. 32; 103; Prov. 17:9; Matt. 6:14,15; 18:15-17; Mark 11:25; Luke 17:3-10; Eph. 4:32; Col. 3:13; Jas. 5:15; 1 John 1:8-10

## Friendship

Prov. 27:6,10; 17:9,17; John 15:13-15

## God's Love and Acceptance

Ps. 27; 103; Luke 15; Acts 27

## Gossip

Prov. 10:18; 11:13; 18: 8; 20:19; 26:20-22; Jas. 4:11

## Grief

2 Sam. 12; Ps. 6:5-7; 23:4; 119:28; 137:1,5,6; Prov. 14:13; 15:13; Matt. 5:4; 14:12-21; 26:38; John 11; 1 Cor. 15; 2 Cor. 4:14-5:8; Eph. 4:30; 1 Thess. 4; 2 Tim. 1:10; Heb. 2:14,15; 9:27

## Guilt

Ps. 32; 103; Isa. 53:6; Matt. 6:12; 18:21f; Luke 15; Rom. 8:23; 2 Cor. 7:8-10; 1 Pet. 1:24; 1 John 1:9

### Causes

Gen. 2:17; 3:4,5; 3:8,22; Job 1:9-11; John 14:26; John 16:8,13; Phil. 3:12-16; 1 Tim. 4:2; 1 John 1:8-10; Rev. 12:10

### Effects

Ps. 73; Rom. 6:23; 1 John 1:9

### Dealing with It

1 Sam. 16:7; Ps. 103:14; 139:1-4; John 8:3-11; Jas. 5:16; 1 Peter 3:18; 1 John 1:8,9

### Preventing

Eph. 4:32

## Habit

Prov. 19:19; Isa. 1:10-17; Jer. 13:23; 22:21; Rom. 6-7; Gal. 5:16-21; Heb. 5:13ff; 1 Pet. 2:14,19

## Homosexuality

Gen. 19; Lev. 18:22; 20:13; Rom. 1:26-32; 1 Cor. 6:9-11; 1 Tim. 1:10

## Hope

Ps. 27; 40:1-3; 119; 121; Prov. 10:28; 13:12; Acts 27; Rom. 15:4,5; 1 Thess. 1:3; 4:13-18; Heb. 6:11,18-19

## Hopelessness, Despair

Ps. 27; 40:13; 103; 121; John 11; Acts 27

## Humility

Prov. 13:34; 15:33; 16:19; 22:4; 29:23; John 13:1-17; Gal. 6:1,2; Eph. 5:15-21; Phil. 2:1-11; Jas. 4:6,10; 1 Pet. 5:6,7

## Laziness

Prov. 12:24,27; 13:4; 15:19; 18:9; 26:13-16; Matt. 25:26

## Life-Dominating Problems

1 Cor. 6:9-12; 21:8; Eph. 5:18; Rev. 21:8; 22:15

## Loneliness

Gen. 2:18; Ps. 25:16; 121; Luke 15; John 11; Acts 27; Eph. 1:3-14; 2 Tim. 4:9-12

### Dealing with It

Prov. 18:24; John 3:16; Rom. 8:9; 8:14-17; 8:26-31; 8:35-39; 1 Cor. 6:19; 1 John 1:9; 4:13

## Love

Prov. 10:12; 17:19; Matt. 5:44; 22:39,40; Rom. 3:10; 1 Cor. 13; 1 Pet. 1:22; 1 John 4:10,19; 5:2,3; 2 John 5,6

## Lying

Ex. 20:16; Prov. 12:19,22; Eph. 4:25; Col. 3:9

## Marital Problems

Gen. 2:18-25; Deut. 24:1-4; Prov. 5:18; 8:22; 19:13; 21:9; 19; 27:15,16; Eccl. 9:9; Matt. 5:31,32; 19:3-9; 1 Cor. 7:10-16; Eph. 5:21-33; Col. 3:18-25; Heb. 13:4; 1 Pet. 3:1-7

### Causes Of

1 Cor. 7:12-16; 2 Cor. 6:15-16; Eph. 5:21-33; Col. 3:18-25; 1 Pet. 3:1-7

## Marriage

Gen. 2:18,24; Eph. 5:22-23; Col. 3:18-21; 1 Pet. 3:1-17; 1 Tim. 3:4,5

## Parent/Child

Gen. 2:24; 2 Cor. 12:14; Eph. 6:1-4; 1 Tim. 3:4,5

## Peace

Ps. 40:1-3; 119; 121; Prov. 3:1,2; 16:7; John 11; 14:27; Rom. 5:1; 12:18; 14:19; Phil. 4:6-9; Col. 3:15; Heb. 12:24

## Pride

Prov. 8:13; 11:2; 13:10; 16:18; 18:12; 21:24; 27:1; 29:23

## Repentance

Luke 3:8-14; 24:47; Acts 3:19; 5:31; 17:30; 26:20; 2 Cor. 7:10; 12:21

## Resentment

Prov. 26:24-26; Heb. 12:15

## Self-Image

Luke 15; Eph. 2:3-14

## Sickness

Ps. 119:71; Matt. 9:2-6; 9:18-26; 10:5-8; 13:58; 25:39,40; Mark 6:7-13; 7:24-30; 9:20-27; Luke 9:1,2,6; 13:1-5; John 9:2,3; Rom. 5:3-5; 8:28; 1 Cor. 11:29,30; 2 Cor. 2:7-10; Heb. 9:27; 12:22; Jas. 1:2-4; 5:1-14; 1 Pet. 1:5-7

### Dealing with It

Rom. 11:33; 1 Cor. 12:25,26; Heb. 11:1; Jas. 5:6; 1 John 1:9

## Singleness

Gen. 2:18; Matt. 19:11,12; 1 Cor. 7:7-28

## Worry

Prov. 12:25; 14:30; 17:22; Matt. 6:24-34; Phil. 4:6,7; 1 Pet. 5:6,7

# Notes

## CHAPTER 2—THE FORGOTTEN PURPOSE OF SCRIPTURE

1. Stephen Prothero, *Religious Literacy: What Every American Needs to Know—and Doesn't* (New York: Harper Collins, 2007), 38.

2. Barna Research Group, "Six Megathemes Emerge," Barna.org website article #462, (Ventura, CA: The Barna Research Group, Ltd., 2010), 2.

3. David Ferguson, *Relational Foundations* (Austin, TX: Relationship Press, 2004), 74.

4. Josh McDowell andSean McDowell, *The Unshakable Truth* (Eugene, OR: Harvest House Publishers, 2010), 36.

## CHAPTER 3—OPENING THE EYES OF OUR HEARTS

1. As quoted by Sean McDowell, *Apologetics for a New Generation* (Eugene, OR: Harvest House Publishers, 2009), 141.

2. Paul C. Vitz, *Faith of the Fatherless: The Psychology of Atheism* (Dallas, TX: Spence Publishing, 2000), 146.

3. David Ferguson, *Relational Foundations* (Austin, TX: Relationship Press, 2004), 45.

4. Gloria Gaither and William J. Gaither, "I Am Loved" (Nashville, TN: William J. Gaither, Inc., 1978), CCLI14019.

5. Ferguson, 57.

## CHAPTER 4—EXPERIENCING JESUS IN SCRIPTURE

1. Adapted from Josh McDowell and Sean McDowell, *The Unshakable Truth* (Eugene, OR: Harvest House Publishers, 2010), 218-219.

2. David Ferguson, *Relational Foundations* (Austin, TX: Relationship Press, 2004), 64-65.

## CHAPTER 5—EXPERIENCING SCRIPTURE WITH OTHERS

1. Adapted from Josh McDowell and Sean McDowell, *The Unshakable Truth* (Eugene, OR: Harvest House Publishers, 2010), 407-408.

2. McDowell, 200.

3. David Ferguson, *The Never Alone Church* (Wheaton, IL: Tyndale House Publishers, 1998), 32.

4. Adapted from McDowell, 268-269.

5. Ferguson, 76.

6. Adapted from McDowell, 404.

## CHAPTER 7—INTERPRETATION: UNDERSTANDING THE INTENDED MEANING

1. Richard Stengel, "Faith, Ever Evolving," Inbox—Editor's Desk, *Time* magazine, April 25, 2011.

2. Jon Meacham, "What if Hell Doesn't Exist?" *Time* magazine, April 25, 2011.

## CHAPTER 11—PLACING YOURSELF WITHIN THE BIG PICTURE OF SCRIPTURE

1. Personal information and study notes of Hosea provided by Dave Bellis II of Copley, Ohio, with full permission to share his story.

## CHAPTER 12—WHY YOU CAN TRUST THE BIBLE

1. This entire chapter has been adapted from Josh McDowell and Sean McDowell, *The Unshakable Truth* (Eugene, OR: Harvest House Publishers, 2010), chapter 9, which was drawn from Josh McDowell, Bob Hostetler, and David H. Bellis, *Beyond Belief to Convictions* (Wheaton, IL: Tyndale House Publishers, 2002), 166-178; and www.seanmcdowell.org.

2. Josh McDowell, *The New Evidence That Demands a Verdict* (Nashville, TN: Nelson, 1999), 74.

3. McDowell, *The New Evidence*, 78.

4. McDowell, *The New Evidence*, 79.

5. Adapted from McDowell, *The New Evidence*, chart, 38.

6. McDowell, *The New Evidence*, 38.

7. McDowell, *The New Evidence*, 38-39.

8. United Bible Society, "2008 Global Summary of Scripture Distribution by Bible Societies," see www.biblesociety.org/index.php?id=21.

9. United Bible Society, "2008 Global Scripture Translation as of December 31, 2008," see www.biblesociety.org/index.php?id=22.

10. Adapted from McDowell, Hostetler, Bellis, 167-169, 176-179.

11. Sean McDowell, "Bones and Dirt," *Apologetics Study Bible for Students,* Sean McDowell, gen. ed. (Nashville, TN: Broadman & Holman Publishers, 2009).

## About the Authors
## and the Josh McDowell Ministry

As a young man, **Josh McDowell** was a skeptic of Christianity. However, while at Kellogg College in Michigan, he was challenged by a group of Christian students to intellectually examine the claims of Jesus Christ. Josh accepted the challenge and came face-to-face with the reality that Jesus was in fact the Son of God, who loved him enough to die for him. Josh committed his life to Christ, and for 50 years he has shared with the world both his testimony and the evidence that God is real and relevant to our everyday lives.

Josh received a bachelor's degree from Wheaton College and a master's degree in theology from Talbot Theological Seminary in California. He has been on staff with Campus Crusade for Christ for almost 50 years. Josh and his wife, Dottie, have been married for more than 40 years and have four grown children and five grandchildren. They live in Southern California.

**Sean McDowell** is an educator, speaker, and author. He graduated summa cum laude from Talbot Theological Seminary with a double master's degree in philosophy and theology. He is the head of the Bible department at Capistrano Valley Christian School and is presently pursuing a PhD in apologetics and worldview studies at Southern Baptist Theological Seminary. You can read Sean's blog and contact him for speaking events at www.seanmcdowell.org.

Sean and his wife, Stephanie, have been married for more than ten years and have two children. They live in Southern California.

# More Resources from Josh and Sean McDowell

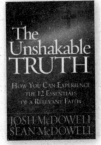

**The Unshakable Truth®**

*How You Can Experience the 12 Essentials of a Relevant Faith*

As a Christian, you may feel unsure about what you believe and why. Maybe you wonder if your faith is even meaningful and credible.

Unpacking 12 biblical truths that define the core of Christian belief and Christianity's reason for existence, this comprehensive yet easy-to-understand handbook helps you discover

- the foundational truths about God, his Word, sin, Christ, the Trinity, the church, and six more that form the bedrock of Christian faith
- how you can live out these truths in relationship with God and others
- ways to pass each truth on to your family and the world around you

Biblically grounded, spiritually challenging, and full of practical examples and real-life stories, *The Unshakable Truth* is a resource applicable to every aspect of everyday life.

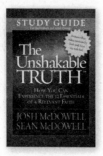

### The Unshakable Truth® Study Guide

This study guide offers you—or you and your group—
a *relational experience* to discover…

- 12 foundational truths of Christianity—in
  sessions about God, his Word, the Trinity, Christ's atonement, his resurrection, his
  return, the church, and five more

- "Truth Encounter" exercises to actually help you live out these
  key truths

- "TruthTalk" assignments on ways to share the essentials of the
  faith with your family and others

Through twelve 15-minute Web-link videos, Josh and Sean McDowell draw
on their own father-son legacy of faith to help you feel adequate to impart
what you believe with confidence. *Includes instructions for group leaders.*

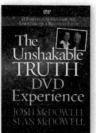

### The Unshakable Truth™ DVD Experience
12 Powerful Sessions on the Essentials of
a Relevant Faith

*What do I believe, and why do I believe it?*
*How is it relevant to my life? How do I live it out?*

If you're asking yourself questions like these, you're
not alone. In 12 quick, easy-to-grasp video sessions based on their book
*The Unshakable Truth*, Josh and Sean McDowell give a solid introduction
to the foundations of the faith.

Josh and Sean outline 12 key truths with clear explanations, compelling
discussions, and provocative "on-the-street" interviews. And uniquely,
they explain these truths *relationally*, showing you how living them out
changes you and affects family and friends—everyone you encounter.
*Helpful leader's directions included.*

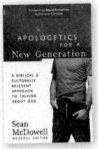

## Apologetics for a New Generation
*A Biblical and Culturally Relevant Approach to Talking About God*
SEAN MCDOWELL

This generation's faith is constantly under attack from the secular media, skeptical teachers, and unbelieving peers. You may wonder, *How can I help?*

Working with young adults every day, Sean McDowell understands their situation and shares your concern. His first-rate team of contributors shows how you can help members of the new generation plant their feet firmly on the truth. Find out how you can walk them through the process of...

- formulating a biblical worldview and applying scriptural principles to everyday issues
- articulating their questions and addressing their doubts in a safe environment
- becoming confident in their faith and effective in their witness

# Take the Complete Unshakable Truth® Journey!

The Unshakable Truth Journey gets to the heart of what being a true follower of Christ means and what knowing him is all about. Each five-session course is based on one of 12 core truths of the Christian faith presented in Josh and Sean McDowell's book *The Unshakable Truth®*.

The Unshakable Truth Journey is uniquely positioned for today's culture because it 1) highlights how Christianity's beliefs affect relationships, 2) promotes a relational, group context in which Christians can experience the teaching in depth, and 3) shows believers how they can live out Christianity's central truths before their community and world.

More than just a program, The Unshakable Truth Journey is a tool for long-term change and transformation!

**CREATED—EXPERIENCE YOUR UNIQUE PURPOSE** is devoted to the truth that God is—he exists, and he created human beings for a reason. It lays a foundation for who people are because they're God's creation, who God designed them to be, and how they can live a life of fulfillment.

**INSPIRED—EXPERIENCE THE POWER OF GOD'S WORD** explores the truth that God has spoken and revealed himself to humanity within the Bible. Further, he gave us his Word for a very clear purpose—to provide for us and protect us.

**BROKEN—EXPERIENCE VICTORY OVER SIN** examines the truth about humankind's brokenness because of original sin, humankind's ongoing problem with sin, and how instead to make right choices in life.

**ACCEPTED—EXPERIENCE GOD'S UNCONDITIONAL LOVE** opens up the truth about God's redemption plan. The truth that God became human establishes his unconditional acceptance of us, which defines our worth. God values us in spite of our sin. This is the basis on which we gain a high sense of worth.

**SACRIFICE—EXPERIENCE A DEEPER WAY TO LOVE** digs into the truth about Christ's atonement. The truth that Christ had to die to purchase our salvation shows the true meaning of love—and how God can bring us into a right relationship with him in spite of our sin.

**FORGIVEN—EXPERIENCE THE SURPRISING GRACE OF GOD** explores the truth about the power of God's grace. The truth that God can offer us forgiveness in spite of our sin helps us understand how we actually obtain a relationship with him.

**GROWING—EXPERIENCE THE DYNAMIC PATH TO TRANSFORMATION** speaks to the truth about our transformed life in Christ. The truth about our transformed life in Christ defines who we are in this world and shows how we can know our purpose in life.

**RESURRECTED—EXPERIENCE FREEDOM FROM THE FEAR OF DEATH** focuses on the truth about Christ's resurrection. The truth that Christ rose from the grave and that his resurrection is a historical event assures us of eternal life and overcomes any fear of dying.

**EMPOWERED—EXPERIENCE LIVING IN THE POWER OF THE SPIRIT** covers the truth about the Trinity. The truth that God is three in one and defines how relationships work through the Holy Spirit lays the foundation for how we can experience the power of the Spirit.

**PERSPECTIVE—EXPERIENCE THE WORLD THROUGH GOD'S EYES** examines the truth about God's kingdom and how it defines a biblical worldview. These sessions show how to gain a biblical worldview.

**COMMUNITY—EXPERIENCE JESUS ALIVE IN HIS PEOPLE** opens up the truth about the church. The truth about Christ's body—the church—provides us with our mission in life and shows us how to experience true community.

**RESTORED—EXPERIENCE THE JOY OF YOUR DESTINY** is devoted to the truth about the return of Christ. The truth that Jesus is coming back helps us grasp our destiny in life and gain an eternal perspective on life and death.

# Other Harvest House Resources to Help You Experience the Truth

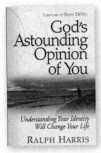

**God's Astounding Opinion of You**
*Understanding Your Identity Will Change Your Life*
RALPH HARRIS

Do you know that God's view of you is much greater than your own? Ralph Harris, founder and President of LifeCourse Ministries, leads you to embrace the Scriptures' truth about what God thinks of you—that you are special to Him, blameless, pure, and lovable.

With clear and simple explanations and examples, this resource will help you turn toward the love affair with God you were created for...a relationship in which you

- exchange fear and obligation for delight and devotion
- recognize the remarkable role and strength of the Holy Spirit in your daily life
- view your status as a *new creation* as the "new normal"—and live accordingly!

*"Reading this book will change the way you think about yourself, God, the Christian life, and maybe a few other things along the way!"*

DAVID GREGORY
AUTHOR OF THE BESTSELLING *DINNER WITH A PERFECT STRANGER*

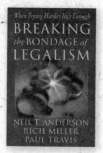

**Breaking the Bondage of Legalism**
*Neil T. Anderson, Rich Miller, and Paul Travis*

The Bible talks about it. You see others experiencing it—a Christian life that goes beyond fearful, grit-your-teeth obedience…a rich, *joyful* life. Here, in the personal stories of many believers, you'll find encouragement to come home to your Father—the One who longs for your presence and invites you to enter into His deep love. Scriptural insights from the authors will help you understand

- the bondage that results from legalism
- God's path of hope and liberation
- the joyful intimacy you can now experience with God your Father and Jesus your Friend

To learn more about other Harvest House books
or to read sample chapters, log on to our website:
**www.harvesthousepublishers.com**

HARVEST HOUSE PUBLISHERS
EUGENE, OREGON